PET Gold

exam maximiser

Jacky Newbrook   Judith Wilson

Contents

Introduction to the *PET Gold Exam Maximiser*

What is the *PET Gold Exam Maximiser*?

The *PET Gold Exam Maximiser* is specially designed to maximise every student's chances of success in the Preliminary English Test examination. It is clearly focused on the PET exam and what you need to do to pass it.

The *PET Gold Exam Maximiser* offers:

- *development* of the important vocabulary and grammar you will need for the exam.
- *the facts* about the papers and questions in the Preliminary English Test examination. The *Exam overview* on pages 6 and 7 gives you information on each of the three papers.
- *step-by-step guidance* and help with all the techniques you will need to use in the exam.
- *specific hints and help* with the different types of exercises in all the different parts of the exam.
- *guided practice* of exam-style exercises, often with hints and tips.
- *special work* on the Speaking paper.
- *help with* correction techniques in writing, especially spelling.
- *a complete sample exam.* This means that you can time yourself, and you can practise your exam techniques as if you were in the real exam.

Who is the *PET Gold Exam Maximiser* for and how can it be used?

The *PET Gold Exam Maximiser* is very flexible and can be used in a variety of situations.

1 **To accompany your Intermediate Coursebook: *Going for Gold Intermediate, Snapshot* or *Opportunities***

You are studying a general English coursebook in class. You are going to take the PET exam at the end of the year, but not all the students in your class plan to do this. Your teacher may use the *PET Gold Exam Maximiser* in afternoon classes for those students who want to take the exam, to give you practice in exam type tasks.

2 **As a short intensive course to prepare you for the exam**

You have been studying a general English coursebook, and your level of English is good enough to take the PET exam. Now you need examination skills and practice, but you only have a short time to prepare. Your teacher can use *PET Gold Exam Maximiser* intensively in the month before the exam.

3 **To help you prepare for the exam on your own**

You can use the *PET Gold Exam Maximiser* independently to give you practice in the exam tasks and how to do them. The *PET Gold Exam Maximiser* gives you clear, easy to understand guidance in exam techniques and clear answers and explanations at the back of the book. You can use the *PET Gold Exam Maximiser* on your own for private study, even if you are not attending a formal class.

How is the *PET Gold Exam Maximiser* organised?

The *PET Gold Exam Maximiser* is organised into 12 units. Each unit deals with an important topic in the exam. The texts and vocabulary exercises in the unit are all connected with this topic. In each unit, there is thorough coverage of vocabulary to give students the important words they need for the topic area. Grammar sections revise and consolidate the language tested in the exam and provide practice in exam format. Each unit has many exercises in the PET exam format, so there is a lot of real exam practice. There are also special sections which give help and advice on how to complete the exam tasks. There is a complete PET exam at the back of the book, which can be used for timed practice.

How to use the *PET Gold Exam Maximiser*

We recommend the following procedure:

- Work through the units in the same order as they are in the book. The grammar and exam preparation work is graded, to introduce students to the exam gradually and give them more help in the early units. Make sure that your students read the *Hot tip!* sections carefully. These give advice on how to do exam tasks, and will help your students with exam technique.

- Work through the exercises in each unit in order. Important vocabulary for the topic is often given at the beginning of each unit, and this will help students with the work in the rest of the unit. The reading and listening texts also contain vocabulary and ideas that will help with the writing task and the speaking practice. It is a good idea to note down useful words and phrases from the texts after reading or listening. At the end of most of the reading and listening activities there are short discussion questions. Don't leave these out! They will give your students useful preparation for the speaking exam as well as ideas they can use in the writing sections.

- The Answer key contains extra help by including alternative answers where appropriate, and explanations as to why certain answers are right. If students get answers wrong, they should try to work out why they are wrong. This will be more useful to them than simply checking the answers with the key. Talk about the mistakes with your students. This will help them to understand what the exam is testing and help them get the right answers next time. If they make mistakes in the listening tasks, the tapescripts in the Answer key can be used to help them see where the correct answers are, and why their answers were wrong.

- Use the explanations in the grammar sections to revise the general grammar point. The transformation exercise at the end of each grammar section shows how the grammar point may be tested in the exam.

- The suggested answers to writing tasks in the Answer key may be used to provide students with ideas for the task, or for comparison with their own answers.

- Use the Practice exam at the end of the book for timed practice under exam conditions. This will give students a good idea of what to expect in the exam.

Exam overview

The PET exam has four components: reading and writing, listening and speaking. They are tested in three papers, Paper 1 (Reading and Writing), Paper 2 (Listening) and Paper 3 (Speaking).

Students have to write their answers on a separate answer sheet. In Paper 1 they write their answers directly on the answer sheet. In Paper 2 they write their answers on the question paper as they listen. They then have six extra minutes at the end to transfer their answers to the answer sheet.

The PET exam tests the use of language in real-life situations.

Reading texts in the exam include:

- street signs and public notices
- websites
- brochures
- posters and guides
- informal letters, emails and messages
- magazine and newspaper articles.

Listening texts are also taken from real-life situations, such as:

- announcements at railway stations and airports
- information given on the radio
- public announcements at sporting events or concerts
- recorded information about cinema programmes.

The student needs to be able to understand factual information in both the reading and listening texts, and also to understand the opinions and attitude of the writer or speaker.

The **Writing section** of the exam tests the student's ability to produce straightforward written English, ranging from producing variations on simple sentences to pieces of continuous text.

In the **Speaking** component, students have to talk about themselves, discuss a problem, describe a picture and discuss their personal opinion with a partner.

Paper	Content	Test focus
Paper 1 Reading and Writing (1 hour 30 minutes)	Reading There are five parts with 35 questions altogether.	
	Part 1 Five multiple-choice questions	• Understanding signs, notices and short personal messages
	Part 2 Matching five descriptions to short texts	• Understanding facts
	Part 3 Ten true/false statements	• Understanding details in a longer text
	Part 4 Short text with five multiple-choice questions	• Understanding the meaning of the whole text and the writer's purpose and opinion
	Part 5 Cloze with ten spaces and four multiple-choice options for each space	• Grammar and vocabulary

Paper	Content	Test focus
	Writing There are three parts with 7 questions overall, including a piece of extended writing.	
	Part 1 Transformation of five sentences	• Grammatical accuracy
	Part 2 Guided writing task	• A real-life task with a strong communicative purpose
	Part 3 Extended writing task: choice of story or informal letter	• A letter or story which is well-organised and uses a range of language
Paper 2 Listening 30 minutes	There are four parts with 25 questions altogether.	
	Part 1 Seven short extracts with multiple-choice questions	• Understanding detail in short conversations and monologues
	Part 2 Six multiple-choice questions	• Understanding factual information in a monologue
	Part 3 A set of notes or a table with six spaces	• Understanding and writing down factual information from a monologue
	Part 4 Six true/false questions	• Understanding meaning, attitude and feelings in an informal conversation
Paper 3 Speaking You will take the Speaking test in a pair with another student 10–12 minutes	There are four parts.	
	Part 1 Answering examiner's questions	• Giving personal information
	Part 2 Discussion of a situation with your partner	• Asking questions, making suggestions, agreeing and disagreeing
	Part 3 Speaking on your own	• Describing what you can see in a photograph
	Part 4 Discussion with your partner on the topic of the photographs in Part 3	• Asking questions and describing your own feelings and ideas

Welcome to my life

Reading

▶ **Part 3**

About the exam

You read a text and decide if ten statements are correct or incorrect.

How to do it

1 Read the statements and highlight or underline the important words.

2 Look for related key words in the text. (These may be the same words, or words with similar meanings.)

3 Decide if the meaning of this part of the text is exactly the same as the statement (*correct*) or different from the statement (*incorrect*).

1

2

3

4

Hot tip!

The statements will be in the same order as the information in the text.

To help you this time, the important words for questions 1–4 and the matching key words in the text are highlighted.

- Look at the sentences on page 9 about a boy called Joe.
- Read the text to decide if each sentence is correct or incorrect.
- If it is correct, write **A**.
- If it is not correct, write **B**.

Back　Forward　Stop　Refresh　Home　AutoFill　Pri

Address: http://joseph–simpson.com

Welcome to my websit

About me:

I'm Joseph Simpson. I was given the name Joseph because it's my grandfather's name, but my family all call me Joe. My friends call me Spike because I've got spikey hair. I'm sixteen, and I was born in London but when I was four we moved to Manchester.

This is me playing the drums at home. I play every day – usually before my mum and dad get home! When I was little I shared a room with my brother Paul. (Bad idea! He's really untidy.) Now I have my own room, so I can keep everything in its proper place. Besides playing the drums I like playing games on my Playstation and reading science fiction.

About my family:

This is my family. My mum is Italian and my parents met when my dad was working in Rome. Then after they got married they came to live in England. My mum still complains about the weather! My brother Paul is next to my father (in the striped T-shirt). He's two years younger

than me. Most of the time we're good friends (except we don't agree about music at all). He's mad about football and his favourite team is Manchester United (of course). My sister Carlie is just eleven, but as you can see here she looks older. She's OK (well most of the time anyway).

Internet zone

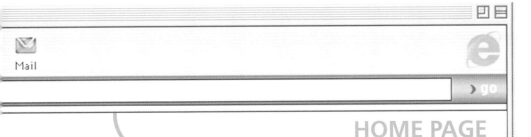

HOME PAGE

My masterpiece

This is an oil painting of my Italian grandparents' farmhouse near Rome. I did it for my art project this year and it took me all term. I copied it from a photograph. We go to stay with my grandparents every year for the summer holidays and I've got lots of cousins round there so we have a great time. This year my grandfather's going to teach me to drive the tractor so I can help him more on the farm.

About my friends:

These are my two best friends, Jas and Pete. Jas is the shorter one with the dark hair. He's brilliant at science and we think he's probably going to be a professor or invent something famous. He's a pretty good singer too. Pete's not so keen on work at school but he's fantastic on the guitar. We're looking for another guitarist so we can make a group. We're all in the same class in year 10 at school, but next year we'll be split up because we're going to new schools.

My favourite quote:

How can I know what I think until I hear what I say?

1 Joe's grandfather is called Joseph. ☐

2 His friends call him a different name from his family. ☐

3 Joe lives in London. ☐

4 He shares a room with his brother. ☐

5 His parents got married in England. ☐

6 He is the oldest child in the family. ☐

7 His grandmother and grandfather live in the middle of Rome. ☐

8 One of his friends is good at science. ☐

9 Joe, Jas and Pete want to find another musician to play with them. ☐

10 Next year Joe will be in the same class as Jas and Pete. ☐

Speaking

▶ Part 1

About the exam

- You and your partner answer questions from the examiner about different topics. These may include your family, your present life, past experiences and future plans.
- You also have to spell all or part of your name.

How to do it

1. Be prepared! Think about interesting things to say about yourself.
2. Don't answer questions with a single word; be prepared to give more details.
3. Learn the alphabet and make sure that you can spell your own name aloud.

Hot tip!

Don't prepare a speech about yourself and learn it as this will sound unnatural. Listen to the examiner and answer the specific question you are asked.

1   Complete the examiner's questions below, using **only** the words in brackets.

1 Where ....?
   (you live do)

2 How ....
   ....?
   (there long lived you have)

3 Do ....
   ....?
   (there like living you)

4 Tell ....
   ....
   (about parents your me)

5 How ....
   ....?
   (and brothers got many you sisters have)

6 What ....?
   (do do you)

7 What ....?
   (hobbies your are)

8 What ....
   ....?
   (doing you in do like evenings the)

9 How ....
   ....?
   (you studied English have long)

10 Do ....
    ....?
    (enjoy you English studying)

2

1 Match each of these answers to one of the questions in Exercise 1.

a) All my life; in fact, I was born there.

b) Yes, it's beautiful, and there are lots of things to do.

c) I'm an only child, but I have two cousins.

d) I'm a student; I'm studying English.

e) Yes, but it's difficult! But I want to travel, so it's important for me.

2 Now think of your own answers for all the questions. Try to think of extra information to make your answer interesting.

3   In Part 1 of the Speaking test you have to spell your surname.

1 📺 To help you to practise spelling aloud, listen to the recording and write down the words you hear. Then check your answers on page 17.

2 Work with a partner. Spell their name aloud and ask them to write down what you say. Then check what your partner has written. Did you spell their name correctly?

Vocabulary

1 Anna is talking about her family. Complete the missing words.

I have three b.................... (two older and one younger) and one younger s.................... so I always have someone to talk to. My m.................... and f.................... both come from large families and so I have many u...................., a.................... and c.................... . I think it's great to be part of such a large family as I'm never lonely and there's always something to do.

2 Which person is Anna talking about? Choose words from the box. (There are some extra words you don't need to use.)

aunt   boyfriend   cousins
grandfather   grandmother
neighbours   schoolfriend
sister   uncle

1 We've always been in the same class at school. We do our homework together and have a laugh. ....

2 I'm very close to her even though she's over seventy. I like listening to her stories about past times. ....

3 We share the same room at home. When we were younger we sometimes used to quarrel, but now we get on really well. ....

4 They live in the house next door to us and we see them most days. ....

5 I met him at a party and we've been going out together for six months. ....

6 We enjoy seeing one another at family celebrations because we're all about the same age. ....

2   Words easily confused in writing

Some words sound the same when we are speaking, but are written differently. Choose the best word(s) from the brackets.

1 I have three brothers and one sister – that makes six of us (all together/altogether).

2 There are (some times/sometimes) when I wish they would all go away!

3 But although we often disagree, we are (all ready/already) to help one another when there's a problem.

4 And I talk to my grandmother (every day/everyday).

3 Angie Brown is filling in information about herself for her class website. She has made seven spelling mistakes. Find the mistakes and correct them.

My name:	Angie Brown
My date of birth:	15th March 1988
My family:	my mother and father, Tim (my older brother), Lucy (my baby sisster)
My favourite place:	the seeside
My favourite things:	my fammily, my freinds, my dog Sammy
Best food:	choclate my mum's aple cake
Best music:	Sky Boys
What I don't like:	cleanning my room, maths homework
My favourite quote:	Don't worry! Be happy!

Internet zone

4   Now write out information for your own website. Use the same headings as Angie. Be careful with spelling.

Reading

▶ **Part 5**

About the exam

- You read a text and choose the correct word for each space.
- There are ten spaces and four choices for each word.

How to do it

1 Read the text quickly first to find what it is about. Don't forget to look at the title.
2 Then read it carefully and think about the missing words.
3 Then look at the four choices and choose the best one for each space.

Hot tip!

Answer **all** the questions. You will not lose extra marks if your answer is wrong.

1   Look at the picture and the questions below the text. Read through the text to find the answers. Don't try to fill in the spaces yet.

1 Who do you think the woman in the picture is?
2 Who is the man?
3 Where did they meet?
4 What happened then?
5 How long did she wait for him?
6 Did he come back?

My grandmother

My grandmother (0) ....is.......... very special to me. I can (1) .... her all my problems, and I love (2) .... to stories of her life. She was born in a small village in the north of England. When she (3) .... 16, the Second World War began and an army training camp opened near the village. The soldiers used to come to dances in the village hall (4) .... weekend. One Saturday a very handsome soldier asked my grandmother to dance. She (5) .... in love with him, but only six weeks (6) .... the soldier was sent to Egypt. He was away for five years but they carried (7) .... writing to one another, and she didn't go out with (8) .... else. And when the war (9) ...., he came straight back to her village and asked her to marry him. That was nearly 60 years (10) ...., and they have been together ever since.

2   Now read the text again and choose the correct word for each space – **A**, **B**, **C** or **D**.

0	A is	B makes	C has	D does
1	A say	B explain	C describe	D tell
2	A writing	B listening	C reading	D hearing
3	A had	B was	C are	D have
4	A some	B both	C every	D all
5	A fell	B got	C became	D felt
6	A after	B more	C following	D later
7	A on	B out	C with	D for
8	A someone	B anywhere	C somewhere	D anyone
9	A ended	B completed	C done	D fought
10	A past	B since	C ago	D long

3   Do you know how your parents or grandparents met? Tell your partner about it.

Grammar

Comparatives, superlatives, *too* and *enough*

When two things or people are the same, we can compare them like this:

I'm as tall as Tim. We're both 1 metre 65.
Rome is just as expensive to live in as Madrid.

→ We use *as ... as* with short and long adjectives.

If two things are **not** the same, we can compare them like this:

1 *Tim was born three years before me. He's my older brother. He is three years older than me.*

→ We add *-er* to short adjectives.

2 *London is more expensive than New York.*

→ We use *more* with long adjectives.

3 *It's less cold today than it was yesterday.*
  Rome is less expensive than London.

→ We use *less* with short and long adjectives.

4 *I'm not as tall as Colin. He's 1 metre 80!*
  Rome's not as expensive as London.

→ We can also use *not as ... as* (or *not so ... as*) with short and long adjectives. This has the same meaning as *less ... than*.

1   Fill in the spaces using the words in the box.

big	cheap	expensive	older
up-to-date			

The red car is just as (1) .... as the blue car, but it's a lot (2) .... Because of this, it's less (3) .... The blue car is more (4) .... than the red car, but it's not as (5) ....

When we have more than two things, we can compare them like this:

Anna is the tallest girl in the class. (She's taller than all the other girls.)

I think maths is the most difficult subject. (It's more difficult than all the other subjects.)

→ We use *the* before both short and long adjectives.

→ We add *-est* to short adjectives.

→ We use *the most* with long adjectives.

2   Fill in the spaces using the words in the box.

cheapest	comfortable	expensive
highest	strongest	

The red shoes have the (1) .... heels and are the most (2) .... The brown shoes look the (3) .... , and the blue slippers are the (4) .... and probably the most (5) ....

Language spot

Sometimes you have to double the consonant:

big – bigger – the biggest
hot – hotter – the hottest
thin – thinner – the thinnest

Some adjectives are irregular:

good – better – the best
bad – worse – the worst
many – more – the most
little – less – the least

When we want to add extra meaning to an adjective, we can use *very*, *too* and *enough*.

This coffee's very hot.
This coffee's too strong – I can't drink it.

→ **too** has a negative meaning

*Is your coffee cool **enough to drink** yet?*

*Those shoes are not **big enough** for me and I haven't got **enough** money to buy them anyway.*

→ *enough* has a positive meaning and *not ... enough* is negative

→ *enough* goes **after** adjectives but **before** nouns

3   Fill in the spaces using the words in the box.

enough   too (×2)   very

I want a computer because it would be (1) ....
useful for my studies. However, my parents say I can't
have one because they're (2) .... expensive and I'd
spend (3) .... much time playing computer games.
I can't buy one myself because I could never save up
(4) .... money.

Writing

▶ **Part 1**

About the exam

- You have to rewrite five sentences.
- You are given the beginning and end of the new sentences. You need to write between one and three words.
- You have to keep the same meanings but use different structures.
- The sentences are all on the same topic.

How to do it

1   Read the first sentence and think about what it means.

2   Read the beginning and end of the new sentence and decide what language is being tested.

3   Think about other changes you need to make, e.g. vocabulary.

4   Complete the new sentence.

5   Check your work:
   Does the second sentence mean the same?
   Have you included all the information?
   Is your grammar correct (e.g. verbs, articles and word order)?
   Is your spelling and punctuation correct?

For each question, complete the second sentence
so that it means the same as the first. These
sentences all practise the grammar from this unit.
However, in the exam the structures will be mixed.
To help you this time, there is a space for every
word you need.

1   My bike was cheaper than my sister's.
   My sister's bike was .... expensive than mine.

2   I haven't got as much homework as you.
   I've got .... you.

3   My sister was born two years before me.
   My sister is two years .... me.

4   I'm not as good at English as my mother.
   My mother is .... English than me.

5   That computer is too expensive for me.
   I haven't got .... for that computer.

Listening

▶ Part 1

About the exam

- You hear seven short recordings.
- There are three pictures for each recording.
- You have to choose the best picture for each recording.
- You hear each recording twice.

How to do it

1 Read the question. Is there a key word?
2 Look at the pictures and notice the differences between them.
3 The first time, listen for key words and think about the best answer.
4 When you hear the recording again, mark the best answer.

---

1   **Exam preparation**

First, do these two examples as preparation for the exam task.

Example 1:
Look at the question. Here, the key word is *When*. Look at the pictures and notice the differences.

When will the boy come to Sandra's house?

A    B    C

🖭 Listen to the recording and fill in the spaces.

Boy If you need the book, I can bring it round to your house tonight. Will you be in?

Girl Well, I've got an English class until .... o'clock but I'll be back about .... an hour .... that.

Boy OK, that's fine – I'm meeting Richard at .... but I can come round to your place first; it's on the way anyway.

Now choose the best answer – **A**, **B** or **C**.

Example 2:
Look at the question, then look at the pictures and notice the differences.

Which photograph are they looking at?

A    B    C

🖭 Listen to the recording and fill in the spaces.

Woman This is me when I was twelve. I had really .... hair then. I wanted it .... but my mother wouldn't let me. And look at those awful .... I hated them!

Man Oh, I think you look nice in glasses.

Now choose the best answer – **A**, **B** or **C**.

2 Exam practice

Choose the correct picture and put a tick (✓) in the box next to it.

1 When will the woman phone Steve?

A ☐   B ☐   C ☐

2 Which photograph are they looking at?

A ☐   B ☐   C ☐

3 Where is Polton?

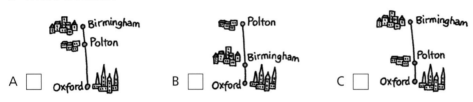

A ☐   B ☐   C ☐

4 Who lives in the apartment?

A ☐   B ☐   C ☐

5 Where is the boy's computer now?

A ☐   B ☐   C ☐

6 What sport does Paul do now?

A ☐   B ☐   C ☐

7 What is the girl's mother doing at present?

A ☐   B ☐   C ☐

Reading

▶ Part 1

> ### About the exam
>
> - You read five short texts. They may be signs, notices, labels or messages. Each text has three explanations – A, B and C.
> - You have to choose the correct explanation for each one.
>
> ### How to do it
>
> 1 Look at the first text. Think about what it means and where you might see it.
> 2 Look at the three explanations.
> 3 Decide which one has the closest meaning.
> 4 Decide what is wrong with the other two explanations.

- Look at the text in each question.
- What does it say?
- Mark the letter next to the correct explanation – **A**, **B** or **C**.

1

> Clare
> The librarian phoned. Your book has
> arrived but you can't collect it today
> as the library closes at lunchtime.
> Shall I pick it up tomorrow?
> Mary

A The library is open all day today.
B Mary can go to the library tomorrow.
C Clare's book is not in the library until tomorrow.

2

> **You must send a recent photograph with your form.**

A Send a photograph of yourself after you send the form.
B Make a photocopy of your form before you send it.
C Put an up-to-date photograph of yourself in the envelope with the form.

3

> Take two tablets with water
> then take one tablet every
> four hours if necessary.

A You can take two tablets every four hours.
B You must take three tablets every day.
C You can take a tablet every four hours.

4

> The competition is not open to company employees or their families.

A You cannot enter the competition if you or your family work for the company.
B The competition will be opened by an employee of the company.
C You cannot enter the competition unless you are a relation of an employee.

5

> People writing to the magazine are asked to include their daytime telephone number.

A You should phone the magazine during the daytime only.
B You should give your telephone number if you send a letter to the magazine.
C You should look in the magazine to find the telephone number to ring.

> ### Answers to Speaking, Part 1, Exercise 3, page 10
>
> London   teacher   brother   hobbies
> study   hospital

UNIT
2 Just like home

Vocabulary

1

1 🔲 Listen to each person talking and decide which room they are in.

bathroom   kitchen   dining room
living room   bedroom   hall   garage
study

1 ....
2 ....
3 ....
4 ....
5 ....
6 ....
7 ....
8 ....

2 Which is your favourite room in your house? Think of two reasons for your answer.

2

1 Make a word to match each definition, using the letters given. Then write the room where you can find this object.

	Object	Room
1 It's a thing for hanging clothes in. (ardreobw)	....	....
2 You can watch programmes on it. (stveleiion)	....	....
3 It keeps food cold. (gdferi)	....	....
4 It's a thing for cooking food. (oecokr)	....	....
5 You use it to keep yourself clean. (rswhoe)	....	....

6 Two or three people can sit on it together. (faos)	....	....
7 The family sit round it to eat a meal. (gndiin tblea)	....	....
8 It's a place to write and to keep your papers. (sked)	....	....
9 It's a place where you can do the washing-up. (nsik)	....	....
10 It's a place for putting magazines and cups of coffee. (fceofe taleb)	....	....

2 Think of one more thing you can find in each room.

3 What's the difference? Complete the sentences with the pairs of words below.

sofa/bed   carpet/mat   armchair/chair
curtains/blind   cushion/pillow   light/lamp
fire/heater   button/switch

1 You find a .... on a bed and a .... on an armchair or a sofa.

2 A .... is usually hard but an .... is soft.

3 People sleep in a .... and sit on a ....

4 A .... is in the ceiling but a .... is on a desk or table.

5 A .... is usually gas or electric, but a .... uses wood or coal.

6 A .... covers the whole floor but a .... just covers a small part of it.

7 You have two .... at the window but usually only one ....

8 You turn a .... to put the light on or off, but you press a .... on a CD player.

Writing

▶ Part 3: letter

About the exam

- You will be given part of a letter from an English-speaking friend or friends. The letter will ask you for some information.
- You have to write a suitable reply, using about 100 words.
- You need to think about
  - what information to include
  - how to plan the letter
  - what language to use.

How to do it

1 Read the task and think about what information is needed.
2 Plan your letter.
3 Write the letter. Remember to include paragraphs.
4 Check your work. Look carefully at spelling, punctuation and grammar.

1

1 Discuss the pictures below with your partner. Describe what each object looks like and say why it would be useful.

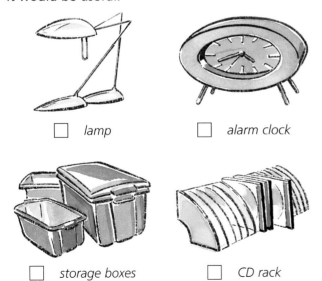

☐ *lamp*   ☐ *alarm clock*

☐ *storage boxes*   ☐ *CD rack*

2 🖭 Listen and decide what object each person is talking about. Write the correct number next to each picture.

2

1 Read the task below.

> **TASK**
>
> - This is part of a letter you receive from your English friend, Tom.
>
> *Yesterday I went shopping and bought a picture for my bedroom. Have you bought anything nice lately? Tell me about it!*
>
> - Write your letter in about 100 words.

2 Now read the letter Kate wrote for this task.

1 Which of the objects in Exercise 1 did Kate buy?
2 How many sentences does she write for each of these points?

Description of what she bought	..... sentences
Why she needed it	..... sentences
What she thinks about it	..... sentences

Dear Tom

Thanks very much for your letter. Yes, yesterday I bought something really nice - a new lamp for the desk in my bedroom. It's made of metal and it's silver-coloured. It's got two legs, which bend just like real legs, and two feet. It's even got a name - it's called 'Mr Jim'.

I really needed a lamp because the light in my bedroom isn't very good. I found I kept getting a headache when I was doing my homework. Now I can see very clearly and I don't get any more headaches. And it makes me laugh because it looks funny!

How are you? Write soon!

Best wishes

Kate

3 Now do the same task. You can write about an object from Exercise 1, or choose something different. Don't forget to check your work when you have finished.

Hot tip!

You can end a letter to a friend in one of these ways:

- Best wishes
- Regards
- All the best
- Yours

Remember to put your own name at the end!

Language spot

Capital letters

Names of people, places, titles, days, months and nationalities always begin with a capital letter.

A new sentence must start with a capital letter and finish with a full stop, question mark (?) or exclamation mark (!).

a) Which of the words below should always have a capital letter? Why?

*london   table   english
mrs smith   book
tuesday   car
july   germany
the sleeping beauty*

b) Add full stops and capital letters where necessary to make two sentences.

It's an alarm clock for my bedroom it's made of plastic and it's bright red

Reading

▶ Part 3

1 What do you know about Australia? Try this quiz. Tick (✓) true or false.

True   False

1 The capital of Australia is Sydney.

2 In Australia, summer is from June to September.

3 English is the main language in Australia.

4 The centre of Australia is mostly desert.

5 The flight from London to Australia takes about 24 hours.

Now check your answers on page 25.

2

- Look at the sentences below about youth hostels in Australia.
- Read the text on the opposite page to decide if each sentence is correct or incorrect.
- If it is correct, write **A**.
- If it is not correct, write **B**.

Remember! *Highlight or underline the key words in the statements. Find the matching information in the text.*

To help you this time, the first two sets of key words are highlighted for you.

1 There are youth hostels in nearly all parts of Australia.

2 Some youth hostels are also used as schools.

3 You can stay in a youth hostel all through the day.

4 Sheets for beds are provided free of charge.

5 Some youth hostels have single rooms.

6 Hostels are more comfortable now than they were in the past.

7 You can stay in a double room in Ballarat.

8 Canberra's youth hostel is the most popular in the world.

9 There are two different types of accommodation in the Undara National Park.

10 There are good views from the Barossa Valley Hostel.

Travelling round Australia

Why not travel round Australia the cheap way? Youth hostelling is an excellent way of seeing the country without spending too much, and the Australian Youth Hostels Association offers you safe and low cost accommodation with hostels just about everywhere in Australia. You can go from a simple country hostel in the middle of nowhere

to a modern new hostel right on the beach. You'll find hostels in buildings that used to be farms, schools and even hotels. There are more than 150 in all, located in cities, the country and places of historical importance. Youth hostels are open for 24 hours a day. They all have kitchens where you can cook your meals, and common rooms where you'll meet travellers from all over the world. Blankets and pillows are provided and you can either bring your own sheets or hire them at the hostel. Overnight fees range from $10 to $24 per person for shared rooms and twin, double and family rooms are also available.

Ballarat

Youth hostels today are very different from the rather uncomfortable hostels of some years ago. In Ballarat, for example, a hostel has been opened in the old town where once people used to dig for gold. The accommodation offers large comfortable rooms at an affordable price. The rooms are suitable for individuals, families and groups, sleeping four to ten people with shared bathroom facilities for both men and women. You are also provided with blankets, limited cooking facilities and heating.

Canberra

Canberra's youth hostel is perfectly situated and the staff have all the latest information about what's on in town to make sure you have a great stay. It is a warm and friendly hostel in a peaceful country setting, with first-rate facilities including kitchens, laundry and plenty of parking. It was

described in the Lonely Planet Guide as 'the second most popular youth hostel world-wide'.

Undara National Park

Undara National Park contains Undara's Tent Village which has accommodation in tents as well as kitchens where you can cook your own food and a dining area with views over the countryside. There's also the Park Hostel, which has low-cost shared rooms together with a restaurant, swimming pool, laundry, gift shop and hot and cold showers.

Barossa Valley

The Barossa Valley Hostel is an old farmhouse, now fully modernised. It has a kitchen with electric oven, microwave and refrigerator. The dining area looks out over the beautiful scenery and there are comfortable living areas with heating.

3   Which hostel would you most like to stay in? Why?

Reading

▶ Part 5

The Story of Icehotel

Icehotel, in northern Sweden, (0) ...*is*.... the world's first, largest and perhaps (1) .... hotel made completely of ice and snow. It has 60 rooms (2) .... a hotel reception, an ice bar, a cinema with ice screen, an ice-art exhibition, and even an ice church (3) .... weddings can take place. And as (4) .... as the building itself, (5) .... inside it – the windows, doors, desks, beds, chairs, tables and lamps – is made of ice. The hotel has to be built again every year.

It (6) .... two months to build; work starts in October and the first guests arrive in December. (7) ...., in late April the ice begins to (8) .... and then the last guests (9) .... out and the hotel turns to water. It is rebuilt the following winter, and (10) .... snowflakes, one year's hotel is never exactly the same as another's!

0	A is	B are	C were	D am
1	A particular	B alone	C only	D one
2	A putting	B containing	C adding	D including
3	A where	B which	C when	D whose
4	A good	B well	C much	D many
5	A nothing	B everything	C something	D anything
6	A takes	B needs	C uses	D lasts
7	A Therefore	B Although	C However	D Even
8	A heat	B run	C move	D melt
9	A register	B go	C check	D leave
10	A similar	B like	C same	D as

1

1 Look at the title of the text and the pictures. What do you think the text is about?

2 Read through the text quickly. Don't try to fill in the spaces yet. Which one of the statements below is true?

a) The hotel sells ice-cream.

b) The hotel is made of ice.

c) The hotel is open all through the year.

2

Now read the text again and choose the correct word for each space – **A**, **B**, **C** or **D**.

3

Would you like to stay at the Icehotel? Why/Why not? Think of three things that it might be difficult to do there.

4   Writing: postcard

1 You are staying in the Icehotel and you write a postcard to an English friend called Joe. Write out these sentences in the best order to make the postcard. Add your own name at the end.

– However, I don't like my ice bed much because it's hard and cold.

– I like the cinema, which has a big ice screen.

– I'm staying in a hotel called the Icehotel where everything's made of ice.

– Dear Joe

2 What three things does your postcard tell Joe about?

Reading

▶ Part 1

- Look at the text in each question.
- What does it say?
- Mark the letter next to the correct explanation – **A**, **B** or **C**.

> **HOUSE FOR SALE:**
> **PHONE 455783**
> **DURING WORKING**
> **HOURS FOR MORE**
> **INFORMATION**

1 A You can only get information about the house at certain times.
 B You can only buy the house during working hours.
 C People are working hard to sell the house.

> **CHILDREN UNDER**
> **12 WHO ARE WITH**
> **TWO ADULTS STAY**
> **FREE IN**
> **ALL YOUTH**
> **HOSTELS**

2 A Children don't have to pay if they are with an adult.
 B Adults who bring more than 12 children stay in the hostel free.
 C Children younger than 12 don't pay when they are with two adults.

Speaking

▶ Part 3

About the exam

- You talk about a photograph.
- You have to speak by yourself for about a minute. Your partner should not say anything.
- Then your partner will talk about a different photograph on the same topic.

How to do it

1 Listen to the instructions. The examiner will tell you what the picture shows.
2 Look quickly at the picture.
3 Describe what you can see and what the people are doing.
4 You can also talk about what the people might be thinking or feeling.

1 Look at the picture below and discuss the following points with a partner.

a) What do the people look like? ☐
b) How are the people feeling? ☐
c) What sort of room is it? ☐
d) What are the people wearing? ☐
e) What can you see in the room? ☐

2 🖭 Listen to a student describing the picture and number the points above in the order in which they are mentioned.

3 Practise describing the picture again. This time try to keep talking by yourself for one minute. If possible, ask your partner to time you. Then listen to your partner and time him/her.

Grammar

Asking questions

> ### Yes/No questions
>
> *Is Carla coming to the party? – Yes, she's coming.*
>
> *Can you invite Tom too? – Yes, I suppose I can invite him.*
>
> *Do you know his phone number? – Yes, I've got it somewhere.*
>
> In a *yes/no* question, an auxiliary verb (e.g. *is*, *has*, *can*) comes at the beginning, before the subject. If there is no auxiliary verb, we must add *do*, *does* or *did*.
>
> ### Subject questions
>
> In some questions a *wh-* word is the subject of the sentence.
>
> *Who* (S) *is coming to the party? – Tom is.*
>
> *Who* (S) *likes Tom? – Carla likes him.*
>
> In these questions, the verb comes **after** the subject, and we don't use *do*, *does* or *did* in the question.
>
> ### Object questions
>
> In some questions, the *wh-* word is the **object** of the sentence.
>
> *Who* (O) *are you* (S) *inviting to the party? – I'm inviting Carla and Tom.*
>
> In these questions, the auxiliary verb comes **before** the subject (but after the *wh-* word). If there is not another auxiliary verb we must use *do*, *does* or *did* (just as in *yes/no* questions).
>
> ### Indirect questions (*Do you know ...*)
>
> Here the words *Do you know ...* tell us that this is a question. There is no other change in word order.
>
> For *yes/no* questions we say *Do you know if/whether ...*
>
> *Do you know if Tom is coming to the party?*
>
> *Do you know when it is?*
>
> *Do you know where they are having it?*
>
> Don't say: *Do you know where is the lesson?* ✗
> Say: *Do you know where the lesson is?* ✓

1 📼 Read the conversation below and complete the questions. Then listen to the recording to see if you were right.

A Is Peter coming with us to the restaurant tonight?

B No, he isn't. I don't know why not.

A Well, ... then?

B Oh, Susie, John and Kevin.

A .... Kevin?

B I think Susie did – she likes him.

A .... we going to?

B The Pizza House.

A .... that? It's so noisy.

B Yes, but it's cheap.

2   Match the parts of the indirect questions below.

1 Do you know who
2 Do you know where
3 Do you know whether
4 Do you know how much

a) the pizzas cost?
b) Susie's coming or not?
c) is coming to the restaurant?
d) the restaurant is?

3   For each question, complete the second sentence so that it means the same as the first. Use no more than three words.

1 Do you know who the winners are?
   Who .... winners?

2 Who is teaching us next week?
   Do you .... teaching us next week?

3 Where was the concert?
   Do you .... the concert was?

4 Are they coming or not?
   Do you know .... coming or not?

5 Do you know what Tim's phone number is?
   Have you .... Tim's phone number?
   HINT: *Here you need to use a different verb.*

Listening

▶ **Part 2**

> ### About the exam
>
> - You hear a person giving some information.
> - There are six questions.
> - You have to choose the best answer from three choices.
> - You hear the recording twice.
>
> ### How to do it
>
> 1 Read the questions and underline any key words.
> 2 Listen and mark the answers you are sure of.
> 3 Listen again to answer the rest and to check.

- Look at the questions for this Part.
- You will hear recorded information about a tour of a famous person's house.
- Put a tick (✓) in the correct box for each question.

To help you this time, the key words in some questions are highlighted.

1 The house at 20 Forthlin Road was bought by Paul McCartney's parents in the
   A 1920s. ☐
   B 1950s. ☐
   C 1960s. ☐

2 The house now belongs to
   A Sir Paul McCartney. ☐
   B Michael McCartney. ☐
   C The National Trust. ☐

3 From October to March the house is open
   A only on Saturdays. ☐
   B from Wednesday to Saturday. ☐
   C from Wednesday to Sunday. ☐

4 The price of the ticket includes ☐
   A refreshments. ☐
   B transport to the house. ☐
   C a tour of Liverpool. ☐

5 Visitors to the house can see
   A Paul's first guitar. ☐
   B the original words of 'Love Me Do'. ☐
   C photographs of The Beatles. ☐

6 Visitors to the house are not allowed to
   A take photographs. ☐
   B sit on the chairs. ☐
   C walk around on their own. ☐

> ***Answers to Australia quiz on page 20***
>
> *1 false   2 false   3 true   4 true*
> *5 true*

Vocabulary

1 The list below shows some things you can do in your spare time. Complete it with verbs from the box.

do	go (×3)	help	listen	read	play	
ride	stay	visit	watch			

1 *listen*.......... to music
2 .... cards
3 .... my bike
4 .... friends and relations
5 .... for a walk
6 .... out to a café or restaurant
7 .... a book or magazine
8 .... TV
9 .... to the cinema, club or disco
10 .... my homework
11 .... in bed late
12 .... with housework

2 Which of these things did you do last weekend? Underline them.

3 Tick (✓) the things you think your partner did last weekend. Then check together.

Example:
A *I think you listened to music and rode your bike.*
B *Well, I listened to music, but I didn't ride my bike last weekend.*

2

1 Order the letters to make a title for each picture below. Write it under the correct picture.

gnsiu a moupctre   ngiatipn a iepcrut

niiksg   gynlipa het atuigr

roahgyphotp

1 ....   2 ....

3 ....   4 ....

5 ....

2 Match the words to the pictures. Write the numbers of the pictures in the boxes.

camera ☐	music ☐	paints ☐
computer ☐	brush ☐	skis ☐
guitar ☐	mouse ☐	film ☐

3 Choose the best picture from Exercise 2 for each of these sentences. Give a reason for each one.

- I'd like someone to teach me how to do this.
- This is something I could do on my own.
- I wish I could do this.
- You need expensive equipment for this.
- I'd like to do this with other people.
- I'm not interested in doing this.
- I think this might be difficult.
- This might be boring.
- This looks the most fun!

Reading

▶ **Part 5**

1 Look at the title of the text and the picture. What do you think the text is about?

2 Read through the text quickly. Don't try to fill in the spaces yet. Which one of the following is **not** mentioned?

a) animals playing games
b) babies playing games
c) young children playing games
d) teenagers playing games
e) games for everyone

3 Now read the text again and choose the correct word for each space – **A**, **B**, **C** or **D**.

The importance of games

Most young animals (0) *spend* a lot of time playing. But they're not just (1) .... fun. They're learning rules to help them grow up safely (2) .... a difficult and dangerous world. In the (3) .... way, children learn a lot through playing games. By playing with toys like balls and building-bricks, young children learn about shapes and colours, sound and (4) .... Once they can talk, children's games are often more social and are (5) .... with their day-to-day lives. They may act the parts of parents, teachers, shopkeepers or doctors – any of the (6) .... they come into contact with. This (7) .... of play is important (8) .... it helps them to understand the adult world (9) .... And playing is not just for children. Games of skill and chance such as card games and board games can be played at (10) .... age.

0	A	spend	B	have	C	tell	D	make
1	A	making	B	feeling	C	having	D	doing
2	A	on	B	at	C	with	D	in
3	A	good	B	human	C	only	D	same
4	A	movement	B	move	C	moving	D	moved
5	A	closed	B	contained	C	covered	D	connected
6	A	children	B	people	C	jobs	D	actors
7	A	length	B	type	C	way	D	work
8	A	even	B	however	C	because	D	although
9	A	better	B	greater	C	longer	D	higher
10	A	all	B	most	C	some	D	any

4 What sort of games do you like to play:

- with friends?
- with family?

Reading

▶ Part 4

- Read the text and questions below.

- For each question, choose the correct answer – **A, B, C** or **D**.

There are hints to help you with these questions.

All4U were once an individual band, standing out from the crowd with excellent CD albums such as 'Saturday again' and 'First love'. Since Steve Simmons left the group, however, they've not been the same. Their recent songs have lacked the special sounds and original ideas that their fans used to expect from them, and there have been reports of disagreements between the remaining band members and even rumours that the group might break up completely. But in their new CD, 'Let's start again', they've started to get back their old magic. There are new songs on the old subject of boy meets girl, and others on wider issues that are sure to get you thinking. Kenny Solo is at his heart-stopping best in 'My girl', and the words and guitar backing to Sam Gold's song 'My lost future' are out of this world. Anyone who's been a fan of their earlier work will be delighted by this album, and if you've been disappointed by their recent work, this will definitely make you a fan again!

1 What is the writer's main purpose in this text?
  A to say what he thinks of a new CD
  B to describe the history of a band
  C to introduce a new band
  D to give his opinion of a new song
HINT: *In this text the writer does three of these things. You need to look at the whole text to find his **main** purpose.*

2 What can a reader find out from this text?
  A what the song 'My lost future' is about
  B why Steve Simmons left the band
  C the name of the band's first CD
  D the types of songs in the band's latest CD
HINT: *Here only **one** of these things is in the text.*

3 What happened to All4U after Steve left the group?
  A They broke up completely.
  B They did not produce any more new songs.
  C They did not have a singer.
  D Their ideas were less original than before.

4 What is the writer's opinion about the band?
  A They're not as good as they used to be.
  B They got better when Sam Gold joined them.
  C Their music has improved recently.
  D They're the best band he knows.

5 Which fan of the band is describing 'Let's start again'?

A

It was the first CD that All4U ever made. They sang some fantastic love songs; everyone who heard it went out and bought it!

B

It's got a great mixture of love songs and songs about other things – some of them are quite serious.

C

The words of the song really make you think – it's not just a love song. And the guitar playing is fantastic.

D

Steve Simmons has brought out a really good CD – the best ever!

Reading

▶ Part 1

- Look at the text in each question.
- What does it say?
- Mark the letter next to the correct explanation – **A**, **B** or **C**.

> ### Hot tip!
>
> It is not enough to look for key words. You may find the same words in the text and in every explanation, but only one explanation is correct. You must think carefully about the meaning of the whole text.

To: Carla
From: Maria
Re: Trip to Golden Sands

Thanks for sending me the tickets for next Saturday's trip. Unfortunately John can't come, but my sister's coming instead. See you then,
Maria

1 A Maria's sister is going on the trip in John's place.
  B Carla did not send Maria enough tickets.
  C John and Maria's sister are going on a trip.

10% discount on book orders of $50 or over

2 A You can save 10% if you order books now.
  B If you order books worth more than $50, you save money.
  C If you order more than 50 books, they are cheaper.

Enter our competition – 500 fantastic music CD prizes to be won!

3 A You can win a prize if you are good at music.
  B Everyone who enters will get a CD.
  C 500 people can win a music CD.

Grammar

> **Permission and requests (+ questions with *I wonder if*)**
>
> To ask permission, you can say:
>
> ***Can I*** *borrow your pen?*
> ***Could I*** *borrow your car?*
>
> To make a request, you can say:
>
> ***Can you*** *lend me your pen?*
> ***Could you*** *lend me your car?*
> ***Would you*** *lend me your car?*

> Which word you choose depends on:
>
> • who you are talking to and how polite you want to be
>
> • what you are asking for.
>
> To make the request even more polite, you can begin *I wonder if ...* This must be followed by *could* or *would*.
>
> *I wonder if I could borrow your car.*
> *I wonder if you would lend me your car.*

1   📼 Read the conversations below and add the missing words to the questions. Then listen to the recording to see if you were correct.

1 Asking if you can do something

a) Informal – talking to a friend
Hey, ... borrow that CD?
Sure, no problem.

b) More formal
.... borrow this CD, please?
Yes, if you're a member of the library.

c) Most formal – often used when asking for something big or difficult
.... borrow your car tomorrow?
I'm afraid I need it myself.

2 Asking someone else to do something

a) Informal
Steve, ... lend .... a pen?
OK. Here you are.

b) More formal
.... lend .... a pen for a minute? I've left mine at home.
Of course.

c) Most formal
Excuse me. .... let .... know when we get to the High Street.
Certainly. It's the next stop after the station.

2   The conversations below have been mixed up. Match the questions to the best answers.

1 Can I sit here, please?
Of course. It's 10.30.

2 Would you lend me your dictionary, please?
Certainly, it is rather hot in here.

3 Excuse me, I wonder if you could tell me the time.
Sure, no problem.

4 I wonder if you'd mind opening the window.
I'm afraid I need it myself.

3   **Writing, Part 1**

For each question, complete the second sentence so that it means the same as the first. Use no more than three words.

1 Can you lend me your dictionary?
Can I .... your dictionary? *

2 Could I have a glass of water, please?
Please .... you bring me a glass of water? *

3 Could I open the window for a minute?
I wonder if .... open the window for a minute?

4 Could you tell me when we get to the station, please?
Would you let .... when we get to the station, please?

*Be careful! *Sometimes when you change the grammar, you also have to change other words used. However, do **not** change the words unless you are sure this is necessary.*

Writing

▶ Part 3: letter

1   Which person is most like you?

A
> I like music with a good beat that makes you want to get up and dance. The words aren't so important.

B
> It depends how I'm feeling. Sometimes I like to listen to sad songs when I'm on my own. But with my friends, I like songs that are more cheerful.

C
> I don't like old pop music like The Beatles sang. I prefer heavy metal and disco – it's more up to date. But it needs to be really loud!

D
> I like listening to traditional songs and classical music.

E
> Some songs are important to me because they remind me of different times in my life.

F
> I like songs that stay in your mind because the music is good and the words mean something.

2   Discuss with a partner.

- What sorts of music do you like? Why?
- What is your favourite song? Why?

3

1   Read this writing task.

> **TASK**
>
> - This is part of a letter you receive from your English friend, Adam.
>
>   *Last week I went to a concert and I really enjoyed it. What sort of music do you like?*
>
> - Now write a letter to Adam, telling him about the sort of music you like.
> - You should write about 100 words.

2   Now write your letter. Here are some phrases you can use.

I really like music that ...
... are my favourite group because ...
One of my favourite songs is ...

> ### *Language spot*
>
> **Punctuation**
>
> When there is a letter or letters missing, we use an apostrophe to show this.
>
> - *I do not like tea. = I don't like tea.*
> - *They have finished eating. = They've finished eating.*
>
> When we use the title of a song, book or film in handwriting, we use inverted commas.
>
> - *The book is called 'Love Story'.*
> - *I saw 'Star Wars' again last night.*

4   The writer has made some mistakes in punctuation in the paragraph below, including apostrophes, inverted commas, capital letters and full stops (see Unit 2 page 20). Find the mistakes and correct them.

I really like Robbie Williams, in fact he's my favourite singer last week I saw him do a great concert on TV there were thousands of people there and he sang some very good songs my favourite is 'angels. Robbie sings a lot of old songs and also some new ones and hes a great performer

Speaking

▶ Part 2

About the exam

- You have to talk with your partner (**not** the examiner).
- The examiner describes a situation and asks you and your partner to talk about it together for about two to three minutes.
- You have some pictures to help you with ideas.

How to do it

1 Listen carefully to the examiner.

2 Discuss all the pictures one by one. Don't agree immediately.

3 Remember to ask your partner's opinion.

4 At the end, you may reach a decision together, but if you still don't agree, it doesn't matter.

Hot tip!

If you don't understand what you have to do, ask the examiner to repeat the instructions.

1 Read this speaking task.

> *You have to help your friend to look after her younger brothers and sisters at home for the afternoon and you will need some things for them to do. Look at the pictures and talk together about what you can do with the children. Then decide which activity would be the best.*

2 Label the five things in the pictures.

3 Read the dialogues below. Write in the missing words. Put a tick (✓) if the speaker is talking about an advantage. Put a cross (✗) if the speaker is talking about a disadvantage.

1 A Well I think the .... is a good idea because all children like cartoons.

   B Yes, and as well as that it would keep them quiet.

   A Yes, but on the other hand they're just sitting in front of the television all afternoon. That's not very good for them.

2 B The .... might be a problem because maybe the children can't read it.

   A No, but we could read to them. Children like listening to stories.

   B That's a good idea.

3 A The .... wouldn't be any good for the boys.

   B But my little brother has one and he really likes it!

   A But it's more for bedtime, isn't it? Not for playing with.

4 📼 Now listen to see if you were correct, and then read the dialogues with a partner.

5 🎙 Listen to people talking about the last two objects. Write in the missing information.

Object ....   Object ....

Advantage ....   Advantage ....

Disadvantage ....   Disadvantage ....

Now talk about the last two objects in the same way.

6 Finally, cover up the dialogues in Exercise 3 and do the Speaking task. Remember you have to decide which object would be best to use with the children.

Listening

▶ **Part 2**

1 Before you listen, read through the questions carefully. How many book titles are mentioned? (These book titles are key words – listen for them carefully.)

2 🎙

- Look at the questions for this Part.
- You will hear a woman talking about books on a radio programme for English students.
- Put a tick (✓) in the correct box for each question.

1 The speaker is talking about reading

   A for homework. ☐

   B in school. ☐

   C for pleasure. ☐

2 What is most important when choosing a book?

   A the vocabulary ☐

   B the subject ☐

   C the writer ☐

3 She says you should also choose a book that

   A looks easy. ☐

   B is just above your level. ☐

   C has a good ending. ☐

4 What type of story is *Look Behind You*?

   A a thriller ☐

   B a historical novel ☐

   C a travel story ☐

5 In *Just in Time* the visitors from space want to

   A ask for help. ☐

   B destroy the world. ☐

   C find Mara's secret. ☐

6 In *Chocolate Kisse*s the main problem for Annie is Pietro's

   A job. ☐

   B mother. ☐

   C schoolfriend. ☐

3 What was the last type of story you read in your own language?

- a thriller
- an adventure story
- a historical novel
- a love story
- a travel story
- a true-life story

Write two sentences about it, or tell your partner about it.

Example:
It was very interesting because ...
I didn't like it much because ...

Get some exercise

Vocabulary

1 Complete the names of these sports.

1 f _ _ _ _ _ _ l

2 h _ g _ j _ _ p

3 b _ _ _ _ _ l

4 g _ _ n _ _ _ _ s

5 h _ c _ _ y

6 v _ _ _ _ y _ _ _ l

7 r _ g _ y

8 r _ w _ _ g

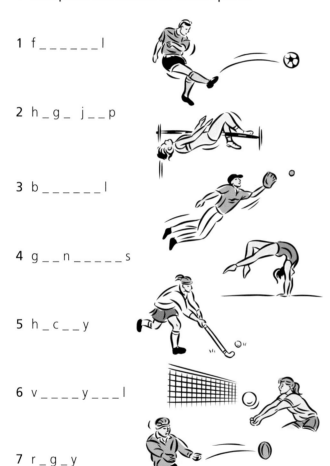

2 Complete the following sentences with a verb from the box. Then match each sentence to one of the pictures.

kick   jump   balance   hold   row
catch   hit   throw

1 You sometimes have to .... on a piece of wood that is only 6 cm wide.

2 You should always .... the stick with both hands.

3 You have to .... over a high bar.

4 The players have to .... an oval ball to one another.

5 Someone hits a ball, and the people in the other team have to try to .... it.

6 Eleven players have to .... a round ball to one another.

7 You have to .... a ball over a net with your hands.

8 You have to .... a boat as fast as you can towards the winning line.

3 Write short answers to the questions below, or discuss them with a partner.

1 Which of the sports above are played in a team?

2 Which one is usually done inside a building?

3 Which ones have you tried?

4 Which ones would you like to try?

5 Which ones would you **not** like to try? Why not?

1 The sentences below describe accidents that happened when people were doing sport. Which sport was each person doing? Choose from the box. (There are two extra sports you do not need.)

athletics   basketball   cricket
cycling   surfing   tennis

1 I was riding down a hill very fast when I hit a hole in the road and I fell off and broke my leg, and I had to go to hospital in an ambulance. ....

2 I was on my board waiting for a big wave. A huge one came and I lost my balance and fell off my board. I nearly drowned! ....

3 I was running on the track and it was wet; I slipped and hurt my ankle. Luckily it was only twisted, not broken. ....

4 I was playing in a match with three friends when my partner accidentally hit me in the face with her racket. The next day I had a real black eye! ....

2 Have you ever been in an accident when you were doing sport? What happened?

Listening

▶ **Part 3**

> ### About the exam
>
> - You hear someone talking.
> - You have to complete notes or a form.
> - There are six spaces.
> - You write 1–3 words in each space.
> - You hear the recording twice.
>
> ### How to do it
>
> 1 Look through the notes before you listen to find out about the topic.
> 2 The first time you listen, think about the meaning and complete as many spaces as you can.
> 3 Then look through quickly. Do your answers make sense?
> 4 The second time, check and complete your answers.
> 5 After the recording (or when you transfer your answers), check your work! Is your spelling correct? Is your writing clear and easy to read?

> ### Hot tip!
>
> You will not get a mark if you write too many words. Never write more than three words for one answer. Often, you only need one word.

- Look at the medical notes below.
- Some information is missing.
- You will hear a doctor talking to a girl who has had an accident.
- For each question, fill in the missing information in the numbered space.

Name of patient: Lucy Martin

Type of injury: twisted (1) ....

Cause: fell during gym lesson

Advice given:

– try to (2) .... the ankle.

– don't (3) .... for the next few days.

– put (4) .... on regularly.

– put elastic bandage on.

– take pain killers if necessary – not more than (5) .... tablets in 24 hours.

Next appointment: seven days' time in Clinic 6 – to be shown (6) ....

Reading

▶ Part 2

About the exam

- You read about five people (or five groups of people).
- You read eight descriptions of objects, places or activities (e.g. videos, restaurants or sports classes).
- You have to match each person to **one** description.

How to do it

1 Read about all the people first. Mark the key information (what they want and what they don't want).

2 Read carefully through the descriptions to find one that matches the first person. Mark this. If you are not sure, put a question mark (?).

3 Continue until you have found a possible match for all the people.

4 Look back at the descriptions where you have a question mark and check with the remaining people. Remember to look for key words.

5 Finally check that you have only **one** description for each person.

Hot tip!

You may find two descriptions that match some of your key words, but there will only be one that matches **all** the information.

- These people all want to do some sort of sport.

- On the opposite page there are descriptions of eight types of sports activities.

- Decide which type of exercise (**letters A–H**) would be most suitable for each person or family (**numbers 1–5**).

To help you this time, the key words are highlighted.

1 Jane has two small children. She wants to meet people and do some exercise while her children are looked after. She doesn't like swimming. She can only go during the daytime.

HINT: *There are **three** places which mention child care or looking after children. Check which place matches the other key words.*

2 George and Jennifer are in their sixties and are not very fit. Their doctor says they need more exercise, and has recommended swimming. They are free during the day and in the evenings. They would like to go together.

HINT: *'swimming' – there are **three** swimming activities. Find the one that matches the other key words.*

3 Jonathan works in an office all day. He's going skiing soon and wants to get fit and make his legs stronger. He'd rather join a class than exercise on his own.

HINT: *'works in an office all day' – this means he is only free in the evenings or at weekends. 'get fit … legs stronger' – there are **three** places where he could do this in the evenings. Check which place matches the other key words.*

4 Sammy is five next week. His parents want a party with the opportunity for lots of activity and fun for Sammy and all his friends, but without the risk of accidents!

HINT: *First find **two** places which match the first key words. Then choose one place which matches all the key words.*

5 David is a serious athlete who wants to be taught by a qualified member of staff. He wants his own individual programme of training in a gym. He wants to train every evening.

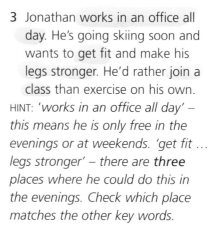

A BODY COMBAT

Body Combat is a complete all-body workout class. The energetic arm and leg movements strengthen your arms and legs, and improve your general fitness. Classes take place on Monday and Thursday evenings and Saturday afternoons.

B

HALL OF FUN

Leave your children here for an hour of supervised fun and games while you swim (ladies only). Children can do ball games and gymnastics with qualified instructors. Unfortunately we cannot take large groups of children.

C

THE SPLASH CENTRE

The Centre provides excellent swimming facilities for all ages, and all abilities. There are swimming lessons for groups seven days a week, including special children's lessons at weekends. On Wednesday mornings and Saturday afternoons there are special 'over 50s' sessions where older swimmers can relax and improve their skills.

D

THE RAINBOW CASTLE

This house of fun is open every day for birthday parties and family fun. Anyone under 12 can use the Rainbow Castle and there are comfortable seating areas nearby for parents. Our trained staff are always there to check that the children are safe. Refreshments are available, and a special party menu can be provided if booked in advance.

E

BODYZONE

Bodyzone is an air-conditioned fitness centre where you can work individually on any of 35 machines. It is suitable for everyone from beginners to experienced athletes. All our staff are fully qualified and will provide a fitness programme designed especially for your needs. Bodyzone is open until 10 p.m. seven days a week.

F LADIES' MORNINGS

Come and join one of our highly successful ladies' mornings every Tuesday and Thursday. Take part in a wide range of activities of your choice in a relaxed and friendly atmosphere, with our team of highly qualified instructors. Child care is available so you can leave your little ones to play safely while you work out.

G

IMAGES

Since it was opened last year, the Images Health Studio has become the top gym in the area. It is fully air-conditioned and has a wide range of equipment from rowing machines to weights, all for individual use. Images is open every day from 8 a.m.–10 p.m. and has its own café for drinks and healthy snacks.

H AQUA AEROBICS FOR WOMEN

We have women's aqua aerobic sessions available on Tuesday evenings and Thursday mornings. Even if you are not a good swimmer you can take part in this activity! Why not give it a try and start exercising now! Child care available for the under-fives.

Speaking

▶ Part 3

Here are two photographs of people doing exercise.

1   Look at Picture A. Think about these questions.

1 Where is the person?
2 What is he doing?
3 What is he wearing?
4 Why do you think he is there?
5 How do you think he is feeling?

2

1 Practise talking about the picture, using the questions to help you. Try to continue for one minute. Work with a partner if you can.

2 Now do the same with Picture B.

Writing

▶ Part 2: short communicative message

About the exam

- You write a short message such as a note, email, card or postcard. You have to write 35–45 words.

How to do it

1 Read the task carefully. It will tell you who to write to and what sort of message to write.

2 Look at the three bullet points and think about what sort of information is needed for each one.

3 Write your message, using complete sentences. You will probably need to use about three sentences.

4 At the end, check your work for spelling, punctuation and grammar mistakes. Make sure that you have included the information for all three bullet points.

1

1 Read the two tasks below. How many things do you have to write about in each task?

TASK 1

Yesterday you had dinner at the house of your English friend, Steve. Write a card to send to Steve. In the card you must:

- thank him for the meal
- say what you enjoyed about it
- invite him to visit you.

TASK 2

You agreed to go to a concert with an English friend, Annie. Now you cannot go. Write an email to Annie. In the email you should:

- apologise for the change in plan
- explain why you can't go to the concert
- suggest someone else who could go instead of you.

2 Now choose the best sentences from the list below for each message and write them out in the correct order.

1

Dear Steve

Best wishes
Carlotta

2

Hi, Annie
....
....
Guido

I've hurt my ankle playing volleyball and I can't walk.

Thanks very much for inviting me to dinner last night.

We could ask Sam if he wants to go in my place – I'm sure he'd like to.

I hope you can come round to my flat for a meal soon – how about sometime next week?

I'm sorry, but I can't go to the concert tomorrow night.

I really enjoyed the meal, especially the chocolate dessert!

2

1 Match the instructions 1–5 to the phrases a–e.

1 thank (someone) for …

2 apologise for something

3 suggest something

4 say what you enjoyed

5 invite someone to do something

a) I really enjoyed … especially

b) I'm sorry, but I can't …

c) Thank you very much for inviting me to …

d) I hope you can …

e) We could …

2 Now check your answers with the messages in Exercise 1.

3

1 Look at this task and at one student's reply. The student has forgotten to include one piece of information. What is missing?

TASK

You are having a holiday by the sea and buy a postcard. Write the postcard to your English friend, Adam. In the card you should:

● tell him where you are
● describe the place
● say what you are enjoying most.

Hi! I'm staying in a place called Cadgwith. It's a seaside fishing village, with lots of old houses and some good beaches nearby.
Hope to see you soon
all the best
Jan

2 Write the postcard out again including the missing information.

4   Now do this task. Write 35–45 words.

TASK

You are going to the cinema tonight. Write a note to an English friend called Jack. In your note you should:

● tell him what film you are going to
● invite him to join you
● suggest a time and place to meet.

Hot tip!

Beginning and ending emails, cards and notes

In an email, card or note to someone you don't know well, it's best to begin and end as in an informal letter (*Dear … / Best wishes, …*).

Writing to a close friend, you can begin *Hi …*, or just write their name. You can end with *Best wishes* or just write your own name.

Speaking

▶ **Part 4**

About the exam

● The examiner gives you a topic to discuss. It is connected to the pictures in Part 3.
● You talk to your partner for about three minutes.
● The examiner listens but does not take part.

How to do it

1 Listen carefully to what the examiner says. There will usually be two things to talk about (for example, what you like and don't like).
2 You will probably need to give your opinions and talk about your personal experiences.

Hot tip!

This is a conversation, not an individual talk. It is important that you listen to your partner and respond to him/her. Don't talk to the examiner, only to your partner.

1   Look at the statements below and complete them for yourself.

I like/don't like to do exercise with other people because …

I like/don't like regular exercise classes because …

I like/don't like sports where there's a competition or a winner because …

I like/don't like to be in a team because …

I like/don't like to be outside because …

I like/don't like water sports because …

I like … because …

I don't like … because …

2   Explain your answers to a partner and find out about your partner's answers.

Example:

A *I like to do exercise with other people because it's more fun to be with my friends. How about you?*
B *Mmm. Sometimes it's nice to be on your own. Especially if you're not very good at sport.*

3   Find a new partner. Cover up Exercise 1 above. Talk together about the kind of exercise you each like to do and the kind of exercise you don't like to do. Try to keep talking together for about three minutes. Remember to ask your partner questions and to sound interested in his/her answers.

Grammar

Ability: *can, could, be able to, manage to*

Ability in the present and future

We use *can* to talk about two sorts of things we are able to do:

a) general abilities

*I **can** swim. I learned when I was eight years old.*

b) particular things we are able to do in the present or future

*I **can** meet you at six o'clock.*

We often use *can* before verbs like *see, hear* and *smell*.

*I **can** see the bus coming.*

Be able to has a similar meaning to *can* but is rather more formal.

*He isn't able **to** see you just now./He is unable **to** see you just now.*

1

1 🔲 Complete the dialogue below using *can* or *can't*. Then listen and check.

A We're all going swimming on Sunday. .... you come with us?

B Well, I'd love to, but I .... I've got so much homework.

A You .... do it on Sunday evening. Come on. It'll be fun.

B Well, actually I .... swim.

A .... you? It's easy. I'll teach you. So you're coming?

B OK, thanks.

2 Complete the sentences below using the correct form of *be able to*.

1 Unfortunately, we .... not .... refund your money.

2 We .... offer you an appointment at 4 p.m. on Wednesday.

3 I'm afraid the doctor is .... to see you today.

Ability in the past

When we make **statements** or ask **questions** about the past, we use *could* to talk about **general** abilities (for example, things we learned to do).

For **particular** actions we use *was able to*. If it was something difficult, we often say *managed to*.

	could/ was able to	ride a bike when I was six.
I	was able to	use my credit card to pay for the meal. (**not** *could*)
	managed to	pass the exam. (but it was difficult)

However, when we use the **negative** we can use all three forms.

	couldn't	
I	wasn't able to	win the game/pass the exam/ ride a bike until I was ten.
	didn't manage to	

---

2   Decide if the underlined parts of the sentences below are correct or incorrect. Change the parts that are incorrect.

1 I <u>could</u> play tennis quite well when I was seven.

2 I found it really difficult to pass my driving test but finally I <u>could</u> pass it.

3 I <u>could</u> pass the exam because I studied hard.

4 After training for five years I <u>managed to</u> win the gold medal.

5 When the ship sank, some people <u>were able to</u> swim to the lifeboats.

3   Writing, Part 1

Here are some sentences about sport and health. For each question, complete the second sentence so that it means the same as the first. Use no more than three words.

1 He can't play tennis any more.
He isn't .... to play tennis any more.

2 Does the doctor have time to see me tomorrow morning?
Will the doctor be .... see me tomorrow morning?

3 I couldn't swim until I was ten.
I didn't learn .... until I was ten.

4 I was unable to get out of the water in time.
I didn't .... to get out of the water in time.

5 Fortunately, I managed to win the last game.
Fortunately, I was .... win the last game.

Reading

▶ Part 1

- Look at the text in each question.
- What does it say?
- Mark the letter next to the correct explanation – **A**, **B** or **C**.

| Danger – wet floor |
| Cleaning in progress |

1 A Be careful because you might slip on the wet floor.
   B Cleaning is dangerous because the floor is wet.
   C Be careful when you are cleaning the floor.

| Before swimming please put your clothes in the lockers provided |

2 A There are lockers provided for your swimming clothes.
   B Don't swim before you are provided with a locker.
   C Lock your clothes up before you go swimming.

Reading

▶ Part 5

1

1 Look at the picture and the title of the text below. How much do you know about football? Discuss the following questions.

a) Where did football start?

b) When did it start?

2 Now read the text quickly and see if you were right. Don't try to fill in the spaces yet.

2   Now read the text again and choose the correct word for each space – **A**, **B**, **C** or **D**.

The history of football

There (0) ....*are*............ records of early forms of football in China at least two thousand years ago. But it was in 14th century England (1) .... the game first became generally popular. (2) ...., it was not like the game we now know as football. The ball was an animal skin filled with wool, the football game took (3) .... all over the town, sometimes with as many as 500 players, and the game went (4) .... all day long. Many games were no (5) .... than street battles, with the players trying to get (6) .... of the ball in any way they (7) .... There were no teams and no (8) .... Buildings were damaged and windows (9) ...., and people were badly injured and sometimes even killed. It was not until 1863, when the Football Association was formed, that the game as we know it (10) .... to be played.

0	A are	B see	C make	D show
1	A why	B that	C which	D when
2	A Because	B So	C Therefore	D However
3	A part	B sides	C place	D streets
4	A on	B at	C through	D up
5	A much	B many	C more	D most
6	A hold	B part	C catch	D kick
7	A could	B would	C need	D must
8	A orders	B rules	C marks	D ticks
9	A lost	B dropped	C broken	D hurt
10	A let	B began	C made	D had

3   What differences can you find between the game played in 14th-century England and modern football?

Something to eat

Reading

▶ **Part 1**

- Look at the text in each question.
- What does it say?
- Mark the letter next to the correct explanation – **A**, **B** or **C**.

> ### Hot tip!
>
> Try to imagine where you might see the text and what it is *likely* to mean when you read the question. This will help you to think of the most sensible answer.

NO SMOKING EXCEPT IN SMOKING AREAS

1 A You are not allowed to smoke in this building.
   B You can only smoke in one area.
   C You can smoke in some places.

BOOK FOR A PARTY OF SIX IN OUR RESTAURANT AND HAVE YOUR DESSERT FREE!

2 A Desserts are free in the restaurant after six.
   B Six people can have a free dessert in the restaurant.
   C Dessert is free when six people book in advance.

Reading

▶ **Part 2**

- The people below all want to go out for a meal.
- Opposite there are descriptions of eight places to eat.
- Decide which places (**letters A–H**) would be the most suitable for each person or family (**numbers 1–5**).

Remember! *First read about the people and mark the key information. To help you, the key information in 1 and 2 has been highlighted.*

1   James likes unusual food from different parts of the world. He is celebrating his birthday and wants to invite a lot of family and friends, including some children. Some of the guests are smokers.

2   Jane is a vegetarian, and doesn't eat meat or fish, but her friend Pat doesn't like vegetarian food. They both smoke. They haven't seen each other for a long time, and want to go out to lunch together.

3   John is a businessman. He never has much time and gets annoyed when he has to wait in restaurants. He likes most English and American food but he hates fish.

4   Andrew and Tina want to go out for an Italian meal with their two small children. They don't want to go anywhere where people will be smoking.

5   Paul and Roger are going to watch a video at home with some friends, and they want some food for the evening. Paul doesn't like Italian food.

A The Curry House

A warm welcome awaits you at the only Indian restaurant in Lonton. We provide a wide range of unusual curries and welcome families in our large non-smoking dining room. Special room with smoking area available for parties. Open from 7.00 p.m. until late.

B New Garden Chinese Restaurant

Chinese food and English fish and chips served in our small dining area. Food is also available to take away at a 10% discount on menu prices. Fast service. Open daily except Sundays.

C Bangkok City

Thai food in friendly and quiet non-smoking restaurant. The atmosphere is welcoming and the food is cooked only when you order it. A wide range of vegetarian and non-vegetarian choices means that this will be a very special evening for you to remember. Booking essential.

D American Burger House

Food served in a moment! Why wait? Check out our prices! Children love our combination burger meals, all served with French fries and a soft drink. We are open from 11 a.m.–11 p.m. every day except Sunday.

E Jo's Place

We offer a wide range of meals, including three different vegetarian dishes every day. Try our speciality beef fillet steak, served with onions and mushrooms, only £5.99.
Restaurant open daily from 11 a.m.

F The Bluebell Inn

This historic building provides a wonderful setting for your evening out. Choose from our extensive menu which includes a variety of fresh fish dishes and Italian specialities. We have a no-smoking area. Unfortunately we do not cater for children.

G Straw Hat Restaurant

It's party time! Come and enjoy typically English dishes, such as roast beef and Yorkshire pudding, and dance the night away. Live music every night except Monday. This is a great place for that special celebration! To book a table phone 01322 467832.

H Pizza House

Excellent pizzas cooked to order using a special Italian recipe, to eat in the restaurant or take away. Our traditional cooking methods mean you may have to wait a little longer, but the results are worth it. No smoking anywhere in the restaurant. Open daily for lunch and evening meals. Children's menu available.

2   Which restaurant would you like to go to?
Why? Complete the sentences below.

I would like to go to … because …

I would not like to go to … because …

Vocabulary

1   Complete the missing words.

1 Carrots, cauliflower, potatoes
and beans are types of v _ _ _ _ _ _ _ _ s.

2 Tea, coffee, milk and juice are all
non-alcoholic d _ _ _ _ s.

3 Rolls and toast are types of b _ _ _ d.

4 Lamb, beef, pork and chicken are all types
of m _ _ t.

5 Tuna, salmon and cod are the names of
three types of f _ _ h.

6 Salt, pepper and herbs are things we use
for s _ _ _ _ _ _ _ g.

7 Oranges, apples and bananas are all
f _ _ _ t.

8 Lettuce, tomatoes and cucumber are
things we often eat in a s _ _ _ d.

2   Odd one out

Which one does not belong in the
group? Complete the sentence saying
why it is different.

1 pasta   ice-cream   cake
The odd one out is .... because it's not
a d _ _ _ _ _ t.

2 butter   cheese   egg
The odd one out is .... because it's not
made of m _ _ k.

3 duck   sausage   lettuce
The odd one out is .... because it's not
m _ _ t.

4 carrot   spinach   salt
The odd one out is .... because it's not
a v _ _ _ _ _ _ e.

5 milk   tea   bread
The odd one out is .... because it's not
a d _ _ _ k.

3   Fill in the missing words. The letters in the boxes spell
a word connected with eating.

1 something you use to eat with   _ _ □ _

2 you sit at this to eat dinner   _ _ _ _ □

3 something sweet you eat at the
end of a meal   _ _ _ □ _ _ _

4 a person who brings your food   _ _ _ □ _ _

5 the biggest part of a meal   _ □ _ _ _ _ _ _ _ _

6 what you read to choose
your meal   _ _ _ □

7 something that goes with a
meal – water or wine   _ □ _ _ _

8 the first course of a dinner   _ _ □ _ _ _ _

9 something you use to cut meat with   _ □ _ _ _

10 money that you leave for service   □ _ _

4   Complete the sentences below with your own ideas.

I have never eaten .... but I would
like to try it.

I have never eaten .... and I don't
want to try it!

The best restaurant I know is ....
because ....

5   Writing: letter

This is part of a letter you receive from your English friend,
Tony.

*We've just been to a restaurant to celebrate my father's
birthday. We had a wonderful meal!
How do you celebrate special events in your family?*

Write a letter to Tony, saying how your family celebrates
special events. Write about 100 words.

Speaking

▶ Part 2

1 Read the speaking task.

> *You are planning a party for a group of friends. You want to have food at the party. Talk about the different possibilities and then decide which one to choose. Use the pictures to help you.*

2 First, think about the advantages and disadvantages of each possibility.

Example:
Well, everyone likes barbecues, but it's hard work.

3 🖭 Listen to two people discussing the party. Complete the information. Are their ideas the same as yours?

	Advantages	Disadvantages
barbecue	everyone likes them	hard work
picnic	• easy to (1) .... • everyone can (2)	might (3) ....
restaurant	(4) .... doesn't matter	too (5) ....
take away	cheaper	• too (6) .... • need (7) ....
fast food restaurant	fun, (8)	not everyone (9) .... fast food
buffet in house	• everyone can have what they (10) .... • can ask people to (11)	a lot of (12) ....

4 🖭 Listen again and complete the expressions the two speakers use to agree and disagree with one another, and to make suggestions.

Agreeing	Disagreeing	Suggesting
• Yes. • I (1) .... so. • That's a (2)	• But … • I'm (3) .... sure … • Perhaps it's (4) .... if …	• We could … • Why (5) .... we …

5 Now work with a partner and discuss which type of party would be the best for you. Talk for about two minutes, taking turns to give your point of view. Use the expressions from the table to help you.

Grammar

Present and past simple passive

How cheese began

Cheese was first made hundreds of years ago, probably by accident. Before the days of glass containers, bags made of animal skins were used for milk. When people travelled from one place to another on horseback, they took the bags of milk with them to drink. The movement of the horse, and the warmth of its body, gradually changed the milk to cheese. People found that this was good to eat, and kept for a long time.

Nowadays most cheese is made by machines in large factories, but some is still made by farmers' wives, who sell it in the local markets.

It is made from the milk of cows, or sometimes from goat's milk or sheep's milk. France is one of the most famous countries for cheese production, and over 500 varieties of cheese are produced there.

1   Look at the highlighted words in the text above. They are all examples of passive verbs. Write each example next to the correct name.

present simple passive ....
.... (am/is/are + past participle)

past simple passive ....
.... (was/were + past participle)

In these examples we are not interested in who made the cheese – there is no phrase with *by ...* after the verb.

2   Find two more passive verbs in the text and underline them.

These verbs are both followed by *by ...* Here it is important to know who or what makes the cheese. This is new information in the sentence so it comes after we have already mentioned the main topic – the cheese.

3

1   Which of the sentences below have passive verbs? Underline these verbs.

1   An unknown person made cheese for the first time hundreds of years ago.

2   Milk was carried on horseback in bags made of animal skins.

3   Cheese was changed to milk by the movement of the horse.

4   It was found that milk kept for a long time.

5   Farmers' wives make all of the cheese sold in France.

6   Nowadays people only make cheese from cow's milk.

7   The people of France produce more than 500 varieties of cheese.

2   Decide if each sentence is true or false. Then check with the text.

Have something done

Linda has lots of money.

She **has her hair cut** in London (by Madonna's hairdresser).
She **has her shoes made** in Italy (by Gucci).
She **has her teeth checked** in New York (by Tom Cruise's dentist).
She **has her clothes made** in Italy (by Prada).

We use the structure *have (something) done* when the verb applies to the noun that goes just before it.

*She has **her hair** cut.*

Here, the verb applies to *her hair* not to *She.*

We use the structure *get (something) done* in the same way. We often use *get* when something is difficult or unpleasant.

*I think there's a hole in my tooth – I need to **get** the tooth **filled**.*

4   Match the problems to the advice.

1 My hair's too long.
2 I can't see the
   whiteboard.
3 My bike is broken.
4 My shoes are dirty.
5 My computer is doing
   strange things.

a) You should have
   it mended.
b) You need to get
   your eyes tested.
c) Why don't you have it cut?
d) You should get it checked out.
e) You could have them cleaned.

5   Writing, Part 1

For each question, complete the second sentence so that it means the same as the first. Use no more than three words.

1 Italian and French food is served in Luigi's restaurant.
   Luigi's restaurant .... Italian and French food.

2 They play jazz in the restaurant every Saturday evening.
   Every Saturday evening, jazz .... in the restaurant.

3 The meals were usually cooked by my mother.
   My mother usually .... the meals.

4 I need to take my coat to the cleaner's this week.
   I need to get .... this week.

5 Our house needs painting this year.
   We need to have .... this year.

Writing

▶ **Part 2: note**

1   📼 You are Dave. Next Saturday you have planned to go out to the Mayfair Restaurant for a special meal with two friends, Louise and Steve. You have just found a message from the restaurant on your answerphone. Listen to the message and complete the notes.

Mayfair Restaurant meal
Time: .... (not ....)
Menu: no .... choice

2   Write a note to Louise. In your note you should:

• explain the situation
• ask her for her opinion
• tell her to contact Steve.

Write 35–45 words. To help you this time, we have written part of the note. Use the words in the box below to complete it. Use capital letters where necessary.

about   be   thanks   could
do   just   no

Louise

The restaurant has (1) .... rung. They want us to (2) .... there at 7.00 not 7.30 next Saturday, and there's (3) .... vegetarian choice. (4) .... you still want to go? If so, (5) .... you let Steve know (6) .... the changes? (7) .... very much.

Dave

3   Now you are Louise. Write a note to Steve. In your note, you should:

• explain about the change
• say why you are not happy about it
• suggest another restaurant.

Write 35–45 words.

Reading

▶ Part 5

1   Read through the text quickly. Don't try to fill in the spaces yet. What is the fruit called? Put the main topics in order.

what it tastes like ☐

what it looks like ☐

what it smells like ☐

2   Now read the text again and choose the correct word for each space – **A**, **B**, **C** or **D**.

A STRANGE FRUIT

If you go to the (0) _market_ in Thailand or Indonesia, you may see a strange fruit. It is about 20 cm long and 15 cm wide, and is covered by a thick (1) .... with dozens of very sharp points. It is called a durian. But what is really (2) .... about this fruit is its smell. This is hard to (3) .... – some people say it's like bad eggs, others say it's like blue cheese, onions and fish (4) .... up together – but everyone agrees that it's disgusting! In fact, it is (5) .... to take durians onto trains or aeroplanes (6) .... the smell makes some people feel sick. In (7) .... of this, if you have the chance you should taste a small (8) .... of the fruit, (9) .... is very rich. You may not like it at (10) ...., but some people think that it tastes wonderful, and call it 'the king of fruit'.

0	A market	B butcher	C baker	D chemist
1	A paper	B skin	C stone	D juice
2	A colourful	B bright	C expensive	D different
3	A buy	B find	C describe	D grow
4	A caught	B mixed	C made	D drunk
5	A forbidden	B told	C meant	D refused
6	A although	B but	C and	D because
7	A way	B spite	C reason	D opposite
8	A piece	B drop	C meal	D half
9	A which	B this	C what	D that
10	A start	B first	C beginning	D one

3   Would you try this fruit if you had the chance? Think of three reasons why you would or would not like to try it and complete the sentence below.

I would/would not like to try a durian firstly because ...,
secondly … and finally …

Listening

▶ Part 4

1

1 Look at the instructions and statements 1–6. Are Katy and Peter:

a) deciding what to order?

b) discussing the food they are eating?

c) talking about a meal they ate in the past?

- You will hear a conversation between two friends, Katy and Peter. They have just sat down in a restaurant.
- Decide if you think each statement is correct or incorrect.
- If you think the statement is correct, put a tick (✓) in the box under **A** for **YES**. If you think it is not correct, put a tick (✓) in the box under **B** for **NO**.

		A YES	B NO
1	It's Peter's first visit to the restaurant.	☐	☐
2	Katy prefers non-smoking restaurants.	☐	☐
3	Katy has plenty of time for lunch.	☐	☐
4	Peter thinks that Katy should order the fish.	☐	☐
5	Peter once got ill through eating beef.	☐	☐
6	Katy is going to order two courses.	☐	☐

2 Now follow the instructions.

2   Before you check your answers, look at the phrases below. Was each one spoken by Katy or Peter? Can you remember the endings to 6 and 7?

1 I've never been here before.

2 I come here quite often.

3 I'm really pleased more and more restaurants don't allow it.

4 I haven't got that much time.

5 I'll just have the main course.

6 You really should try ...

7 I got ill once on holiday when I ate ...

8 I'll have a starter.

Now look at your answers to Exercise 1.2 again.

3   Writing: story

Write a story called *A holiday problem*. Write about 100 words. Before you begin, think about these questions.

- When did it happen?
- Where were you?
- What caused the problem?
- How did you feel?
- What happened in the end?

Shopping

Vocabulary

1 Read the sentences below and complete the plan of the department store.

The women's clothing is on the first floor.

Lighting is in the basement.

Luggage is on the ground floor.

Children's clothing is on the floor above women's clothing.

Kitchen equipment is on the same floor as lighting.

The restaurant is right at the top of the building.

Accessories such as scarves and umbrellas are on the same floor as the luggage.

Children's toys are on the same floor as children's clothing.

When you come in off the street, the first thing you see is the make-up counter.

Men's clothing is on the third floor.

Furniture is on the next floor up after the men's clothing.

Soft furnishings are on the same floor as furniture.

The accounts department is near the men's clothing.

Electrical goods are down in the basement.

2

1 These are the things on Stella's shopping list. She can buy eight of them in the department store. Tick (✓) them and write the floor she should go to.

2 There are four more things on Stella's list. Choose the shops where she can buy these things and write them on the list above.

| book shop | greengrocer's | butcher's |
| jeweller's | chemist's | shoe shop |

In the department store

fifth floor

(1) ....

fourth floor

(2) .... (3) ....

third floor

(4) .... (5) ....

second floor

(6) .... (7) ....

first floor

(8) ....

ground floor

(9) .... (10) .... (11) ....

basement

(12) .... (13) .... (14) ....

socks (for Peter)   ....
lipstick   ....
bedside lamp   ....
cough medicine   ....
handbag   ....
dictionary   ....
apples   ....
teddy bear   ....
tie (for grandad)   ....
sofa   ....
sausages   ....
cushion   ....

3   🔊 Listen to the people. Which shop is each person in?

	A	B	C
1	A clothes shop	B shoe shop	C furniture shop
2	A baker's	B book shop	C shoe shop
3	A baker's	B chemist's	C sweet shop
4	A chemist's	B book shop	C supermarket
5	A flower shop	B sweet shop	C baker's
6	A flower shop	B clothes shop	C greengrocer's
7	A baker's	B butcher's	C chemist's
8	A supermarket	B chemist's	C book shop
9	A book shop	B supermarket	C sweet shop
10	A supermarket	B butcher's	C flower shop

4

1 What were the last five things you bought in a shop? Make a list of the things and where you bought them.

2 Which shops you like best? Why? Discuss with a partner.

Speaking

▶ **Part 3**

1   Use the words in the box to help you describe the pictures.

postcard   fruit   piles   cap   pay   jacket
ripe   bag   choose   wear   quality   price
curly   stall   fresh

2   🔊 Listen to extracts from a description of the first picture. Is each statement true or false?

1 ☐   2 ☐   3 ☐
4 ☐   5 ☐   6 ☐

3

Now work with a partner. Describe the first picture to your partner. Try to keep talking for about one minute. After that, your partner should talk about the second picture.

▶ **Part 4**

Your photographs showed people shopping in different places. Now, I'd like you to talk together about the kinds of shopping you enjoy doing, and the kinds of shopping you don't enjoy doing.

1   Look at the speaking task above. Are the following statements about the task correct or incorrect?

1 You must only talk about the kind of shopping you enjoy doing.

2 You must discuss your partner's ideas as well as your own.

3 You must give a list of the different places where you go shopping.

2

1 To help you with this speaking task, first complete the table below with your own ideas.

kind of shopping	things I like about it	things I don't like
food and drink	meet people	always the same
presents	nice to choose something for someone else	
clothes for myself		
holiday souvenirs		
....		
....		

2 Find a partner and compare your ideas. Do you like the same kinds of shopping?

3   Find a new partner. Cover the table above and talk with your partner about the task for about three minutes. (Time yourselves!) Make sure you ask your partner about their ideas as well as telling them yours. Remember to sound interested!

Writing

▶ Part 3: letter

1   Choose the best preposition to complete the sentences below. Use the map to help you.

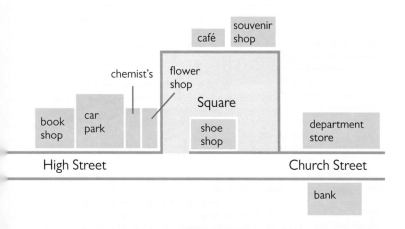

1 The café is .... the square, ... the souvenir shop.

2 The car park is .... the High Street, ... the book shop and the chemist's.

3 The flower shop is .... the chemist's, ... the corner of the square.

4 The shoe shop is .... the square, ... the café.

5 The department store is .... Church Street, ... the bank.

6 The bank is .... Church Street, ... the square.

2   The sentences below all have spelling mistakes. Two sentences also have a mistake in punctuation. Find the mistakes and correct them.

1 The new shop is oposite the post ofice, next to the baker's.

2 It sells realy nice cloths for teenager's.

3 I like it because the peple who work there are very freindly.

4 Also their is music playing and this is fun to lisen to.

5 I boght a new jackit there last week and I love it.

6 Its warm and confortable and it wasn't very excpensive.

3   The sentences below all have a mistake with past or present tense verbs. Find the mistakes and correct them.

1 The new shop sell CDs, videos and DVDs.

2 I like it because the people is very friendly.

3 The shop is very well design and very clean.

4 I am buy a new CD there last week.

5 It was not costing too much money, because it was reduced.

4

1 Read this writing task.

TASK

● This is part of a letter you receive from your English penfriend.

> I've just been shopping with my brother. We went to a new book shop. It was great!
> Do you have any good shops in your town? What are they like?

● Now write a letter to your penfriend, telling him or her about shopping in your town. Write about 100 words.

2 Here are some ideas you could write about. Write notes about each one.

– Where the best shops are (e.g. in the square / in the old town)

– A new shop (what it sells / what you think of it)

– Your favourite shop (why you like it / something you bought there)

5   Now do the task.

Hot tip!

Think of a name for your penfriend (e.g. Tom, Sarah). **Don't** begin ~~Dear friend~~.

Grammar

Conditionals

Zero conditional

When the sun shines, people feel happy.
If it's cold and rainy, they feel sad.

These things apply to a long period of time – past, present and future. They are 'general truths'.

Both parts of the sentence use the present tense.

We can use *when* or *if* to mean 'every time it happens'.

The two halves of the sentence can be in either order.

1   Match the sentence halves.

1 When people don't eat the right food,
2 If you heat ice,
3 When children are bored,
4 If animals have regular exercise,

a) they stay healthy.
b) they get ill.
c) it turns to water.
d) they often behave badly.

First conditional

If it's sunny tomorrow, we'll go to the beach.

When we talk about something possible (but not certain) in the future we use the future in one part of the sentence (e.g. *we'll go to the beach*) and *if* + present in the other part (*if it's sunny*).

When we think something is certain to happen, we use *when* instead of *if*.
***If** I see Sally, I'll tell her.* (I may see Sally but I'm not sure.)
***When** I see Sally, I'll tell her.* (I'm sure I'll see Sally.)

2   Complete the sentences. Give true information. Remember to write about things that are possible!

1 When I get home tonight, I'll …
2 I'll watch television tonight if …
3 If …, I'll be disappointed.
4 I'll be very happy when …

Second conditional

If I won lots of money, I'd travel round the world.

When we talk about something impossible or unlikely in the future, we use *would* + infinitive verb in one part of the sentence (*I'd travel …*) and *if* + the past simple tense in the other part (*if I won …*).

3   Listen to the people talking about what they'd do if they had lots of money, and complete the sentences.

If Paul had lots of money, he'd .... and …
If Annie had lots of money, she'd .... and …
If Josie had lots of money, she'd .... and …
If Don had lots of money, he'd .... and …

Unless

*People are not healthy **unless** they have enough food.*
*I'll probably pass the exam **unless** the questions are awful.*
*I couldn't go round the world **unless** I had lots of money.*

In sentences like this, we can use *unless* instead of *if … not*.

4 Choose the best word to complete each sentence.

1 I won't go out *unless/if* it stops raining.

2 She would be really pleased *unless/if* he passed the exam.

3 *Unless/If* the television is mended they won't be able to watch the football.

4 They wouldn't be able to buy a computer *unless/if* it was cheap.

5 Writing, Part 1

Here are some sentences about shopping in a big city. They practise all the conditionals introduced in this unit. For each question, complete the second sentence so that it means the same as the first. Use no more than three words.

1 Parking is impossible if you arrive late.
It is impossible to park .... you arrive early.

2 You don't have many shops to choose from unless you go to a city.
You have a lot of shops to choose from .... to a city.

3 Fruit is cheaper in the market.
Fruit is cheaper .... you buy it in the market.

4 It's possible that I'll buy that book for Susan – if I do, I'll tell you.
I'll tell you if .... that book for Susan.

5 We might miss the last train – then we'd have to walk home.
We'd have to walk home if we .... the last train.

Reading

▶ **Part 5**

1 Look at the title and read the text below without filling in any of the spaces yet. Is the text about someone who:

a) keeps mice as pets?

b) has a problem with mice?

c) wants to have a mouse?

2

• Read the text below and choose the correct word for each space.

• For each question, mark the letter next to the correct answer – **A**, **B**, **C** or **D**.

A CURE FOR MICE?

We lived (0) ..*in*.. an old house. It was big and comfortable, but there was one problem – mice! The house was (1) .... of them. Then my sister saw a small (2) .... in a magazine. It said, 'Do you want a mouse-free house? For only £10.00 we will send you a (3) .... of equipment which never fails to work!

We (4) .... you it will be 100% successful (5) .... you follow our instructions!'

Well, my sister thought this looked wonderful and she immediately (6) .... off her £10.00. Two days (7) .... a small parcel arrived. My sister unwrapped it excitedly. (8) .... it there were two square blocks of wood, (9) .... A and B, and a small sheet of paper. On the paper were the instructions: 'Place mouse on block A. Hit mouse hard with block B.'

We (10) .... almost hear the mice laughing at us.

0	A in	B on	C at	D up
1	A complete	B full	C crowded	D made
2	A notice	B sign	C advertisement	D picture
3	A piece	B part	C quality	D make
4	A say	B promise	C know	D tell
5	A as	B so	C if	D unless
6	A sent	B threw	C dropped	D gave
7	A since	B next	C more	D later
8	A Outside	B On	C Inside	D Under
9	A marked	B written	C called	D shaped
10	A can	B could	C will	D might

3 Have you, or has anyone in your family, ever bought anything that was surprising or disappointing? Write a sentence about it or tell your partner about it.

Reading

▶ Part 4

Remember! *Question 1 is always about the **writer**. You need to think about what the writer is trying to do in the text. Question 2 is always about the **reader**. What can the reader **find out** from this text? You may need to think about the main idea or a detail.*

> ### Hot tips!
>
> Question 3 may ask you someone's opinion. You have to guess this from the information in the text.
>
> Question 4 may ask you about a detail. You have to read one part of the text very carefully.
>
> For Question 5 you have to think about which answer – **A**, **B**, **C** or **D** – matches the main idea of the text.

- Read the text and questions below.
- For each question, mark the letter next to the correct answer – **A**, **B**, **C** or **D**.

A customer's complaint

Shops are full of attractive things to buy these days. But what are we actually paying for? I recently bought a large packet of chocolate biscuits of a brand I hadn't tried before. When I
5 opened it, I found each biscuit was wrapped individually in silver paper, then they were wrapped together in more paper, and then packed in a strong cardboard box, which was in turn wrapped in plastic! By the time I had actually got at the
10 biscuits, the table was covered in paper and I wasn't hungry any more. (This was probably just as well, as there were only eight biscuits in the packet.) And children's toys are even worse. It was my three-year-old son's birthday last week and at first
15 he was excited to see so many presents all for him! But at the end of the party, when he had finally got through all the wrapping paper, cardboard boxes and plastic bags that they came in, he was too tired to play with any of them. Some of them were so
20 well wrapped that he never did manage to open them, and when I tried to do it for him, I broke my fingernails. I hate to think of the amount of money all of this costs – and who ends up paying? The customer, that's who!

1 What is the writer trying to do in this text?
   A complain that supermarket food is unhealthy
   B complain that children get too many toys
   C complain that many things are too well wrapped
   D complain that everything is too expensive nowadays

2 What can the reader learn from this text?
   A A large packet might not contain much food.
   B It is best to buy food of a well-known brand.
   C It is important to keep food clean and dry.
   D Some food should not be given to very young children.

3 How did the writer's child feel at the end of his birthday party?
   A He was disappointed with his presents.
   B He was looking forward to playing with his presents.
   C He was uninterested in his presents.
   D He was excited about his presents.
   HINT: *Think about what happened when he tried to open the presents. How did this make him feel? (lines 18 to 19)*

4 How did the writer break her fingernails?
   A playing with her son
   B clearing away the rubbish
   C opening a parcel
   D mending a broken toy
   HINT: *Look at the highlighted word in line 21. What did the woman try to do? You need to look back to something earlier.*

5 Which statement would the writer agree with?

   A *I think some packaging is dangerous for young children.*

   B *I like unwrapping things – it's always nice to get a surprise.*

   C *I think that buying special paper to wrap presents in is a waste of money.*

   D *I'd rather buy things which don't have much packaging.*

   HINT: *What idea connects the story about the chocolate biscuits and the story about the birthday presents?*

Listening

▶ Part 1

- There are seven questions in this Part.
- For each question there are three pictures and a short recording.
- You will hear each recording twice.
- For each question, look at the pictures and listen to the recording.
- Choose the correct picture and put a tick (✓) in the box next to it.

Hot tip!

Remember the information you need might **not** be the last thing mentioned in the conversation.

---

1 Where is the post office?

A ☐

B ☐

C ☐

2 What did the man buy Sarah?

A ☐

B ☐

C ☐

3 What is causing the traffic problem?

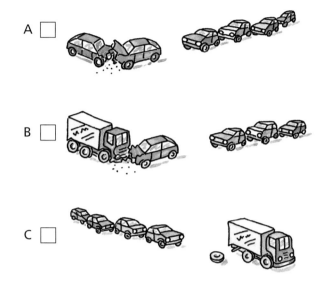

A ☐

B ☐

C ☐

4 What will the man and woman have for lunch?

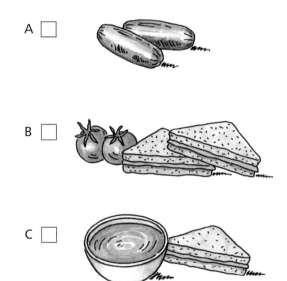

A ☐

B ☐

C ☐

5 What does the woman decide to do with her friend the next day?

A

B

C

6 Where are the woman's car keys?

A

B

C

7 Where did the man hurt himself?

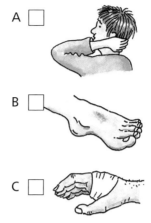

A ☐

B ☐

C ☐

Reading

▶ **Part 1**

- Look at the text in each question.
- What does it say?
- Mark the letter next to the correct explanation – **A**, **B** or **C**.

> **10% DISCOUNT FOR STUDENTS WHEN THEY SHOW A STUDENT CARD**

1 A Students must show a card when they buy anything.

  B Students can get a discount when they buy a card.

  C If students show their card, they pay less.

> **LONGER OPENING HOURS DURING WINTER SALES**

2 A The shop is open for more hours during the winter sales.

  B The shop opens later during the winter sales.

  C The shop closes earlier in the winter.

Going on holiday

Vocabulary

 1

1 There are nine words hidden in the box. They are all things people do on holiday. Use the pictures to help you find the words. Then write the correct word under each picture.

S	F	D	A	N	C	E	Z	S
I	C	I	F	G	K	M	T	U
G	G	U	S	C	T	R	T	N
H	E	E	B	H	Y	E	R	B
T	R	X	S	V	H	L	A	A
S	D	P	Y	W	A	A	V	T
E	G	L	I	H	I	X	E	H
E	J	O	C	P	D	M	L	E
V	M	R	B	D	F	M	V	I
N	I	E	H	C	Y	C	L	E

1 ..*fish*..................   2 ....

3 ....   4 ....

5 ....   6 ....

7 ....   8 ....

9 ....

2 What do you like doing best when you are on holiday? Tell a partner. Use words from the list in Exercise 1.1 and your own ideas.

Example:
I really enjoy ...ing when I'm on holiday.
I quite like ...ing.
I don't like ...ing much because ...
I don't like ...ing at all because ...

 2

1 Put the words from the list below into what you think is the best column.

postcard   sun-cream   bottle of water
T-shirt   picture   necklace   sun hat
scarf   book   guidebook

something to send/give to someone else	a souvenir for me to keep	something I need on holiday

2 Now listen to some people talking about why they buy these things on holiday. Are their ideas the same as yours?

Listening

▶ Part 3

- Look at the notes about an English Adventure Course.
- Some information is missing.
- You will hear an organiser giving someone information about the course on the telephone.
- For each question, fill in the missing information in the numbered space.

1

1 Before you listen, read through the notes.
Are the notes:

a) an application form for a course?

b) information about a course?

2 Look at each space and decide what sort of information you have to give. Choose a) or b).

1 a) course content   b) date
2 a) time   b) type of activity
3 a) activity   b) price
4 a) type of trip   b) price
5 a) date   b) cost
6 a) place to contact   b) person to contact

3 Now listen, and fill in the missing information.

> **Hot tip!**
>
> Fill in all the spaces. You will not lose any extra marks if you try, but get the answer wrong.

4 Look at the notes again. Were your answers to Exercise 1.2 correct?

2   Would you like to go on this course? Think of two things you would enjoy about it.

3   You decide to find out more about the course. Write an email to the organisers. In your email, you should:

- tell them your age and nationality
- say **why** you are interested in the course
- ask about the accommodation.

Write 35–45 words.

English Adventure Course

Course includes:

Mornings
- (1) ....
- projects

Afternoons
(2) .... activities

Evenings
discos, karaoke, (3) ...., etc.

Weekends
Choice of three adventure trips each weekend:
- Lake District Adventure
- (4) ....
- The London Experience

Dates:
12–30 June   Fee: £1,425
13–26 August Fee: (5) £...................
To book a course, contact the (6) ....
department.

Writing

▶ Part 3: letter

1 📼 Sam is on an adventure holiday. He phones his parents to tell them what he's doing. Listen to the conversation and tick (✔) the four things that he's done.

1 ☐

2 ☐

3 ☐

4 ☐

5 ☐

2

1 Read the writing task below and the notes that one student has made.

TASK

• This is part of a letter you receive from your English friend, Ken.

I've just got back from holiday. I had a really good time.
What did you do on your holiday?

• Now write a letter to Ken, telling him what you did on holiday. Write about 100 words.

adventure holiday
nervous at first
tent with three people
canoeing
beach picnic
best thing – rock climbing

2 Here are the sentences the student used in his letter. There are two mistakes (spelling or grammar) in each sentence. Find the mistakes and correct them.

a) I had good time too – I went on an adventur holiday.

b) I was a bit frighten because it was very high, but we had ropes and the instructor help us.

c) Thank for yours letter.

d) It was great holliday!

e) The first day we went canoeing in the see and then we had a fire on the beach and a picknic.

f) At first I felt nerves because I didn't know anyone but I soon maked some friends.

g) The best thing is rock climing.

h) I'm glad you are enjoyed your holliday.

i) I was in tent with three other peoples.

3 Write out the corrected phrases in the right order to make the letter. Use the notes in Exercise 2.1 to help you.

Grammar

Present perfect

I've been there.
I've bought the T-shirt.
I haven't done anything else.
Have you seen anything?
Yes, I have.
No, I haven't.

Remember! *I, you, we, they* **have** + past participle

he, she, it **has** + past participle

1

1 Fill in the spaces using the present perfect. Use short forms where possible. Then match the questions and answers.

1 .... you **ever** seen a tiger?	a) No, but my brother'.......... been to California.
2 .... Carla finished her homework **yet**?	b) They'.......... been here **for** three years.
3 How long .... Helen and Kate been at this school?	c) I'.......... **just** put them in the washing machine. Do you need them now?
4 .... anyone in your family ever been to New York?	d) Yes I .... but only in a zoo. I'.......... **never** seen one in the wild.
5 .... Dave had that cough long?	e) Yes, he'.......... had it **since** the beginning of last week.
6 Where .... you put my football things?	f) No, she .... n't even started it!

2 📼 Listen and check your answers. Then practise saying the questions and answers.

2   The table below shows when we use the present perfect tense. Complete the middle column by adding two examples from the table in Exercise 1.1 (question and answer) for each use. Then add the time words (use the examples to help you).

Use	Example	Time words
a) experiences in the past (we're not interested in the details)	1 and	Have you .... been? No, I've .... been.
b) things which happened in the past (usually recently) where we are interested in the result now	.... and	Have you been ....? I've .... been. I've **already** been.
c) things which began in the past and are still true now	.... and	.... four o'clock .... four years

Be careful! We use *since* when we say the date or time when something began.
We use *for* when we say how long something has continued.

*Carla and I have been friends **since** the day we started school.*
*Carla and I have been friends **for** seven years.*

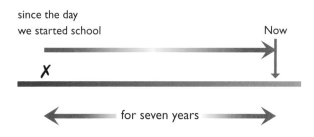

since the day
we started school   Now

X

for seven years

3 Fill in the spaces using words from the box.

> already   ever   for   just   never
> since   yet

1 This is the first time that I've .... stayed up all night.

2 I've been here .... six o'clock. Where on earth have you been?

3 'Why are you looking so happy?' 'I've .... heard I've passed my exam!'

4 She's .... eaten fish in her life and I don't think she'll start now.

5 I've been living in this town .... ten years.

6 'Hasn't that programme finished ....? It's time you did your homework.'
   'I've .... done it! I did it as soon as I got home.'

Past simple or present perfect?

When we say **when** something started, we use the past simple.

When we say **how long** it's continued for, we use the present perfect.

a) We **became** friends when we started school. (past simple)

b) Carla and I **have been** friends since we started school. (present perfect)

a) We **became** friends seven years ago. (past simple)

b) Carla and I **have been** friends for seven years. (present perfect)

The pairs of sentences have similar meanings, but the tenses and time expressions are different, and a different verb is used (be/become). We can use for with both tenses.

My uncle **worked** in London for a year, then he resigned from his job. (for = up to a time in the past)

I **have lived** here for six years. (for = up to and including the present time)

---

4 Choose the correct verb and write it in the correct tense.

1 *start, work*

a) I .... here for a year.

b) I .... this job a year ago.

2 *know, meet*

a) I .... her for years.

b) I .... her years ago.

3 *be, not + leave*

a) She .... still here.

b) She .... yet.

4 *be, go*

a) I .... there before.

b) I .... there a week ago.

5 **Writing, Part 1**

Here are some sentences about people on holiday. For each question, complete the second sentence so that it means the same as the first. Use no more than three words.

1 The last time Paula went on holiday was two years ago.
   Paula hasn't .... for two years.

2 She hasn't visited the art galleries in Rome yet.
   She .... hasn't visited the art galleries in Rome.

3 I finished writing the postcard a minute ago.
   I've .... finished writing the postcard.

4 Jaime hasn't been to England before.
   This is the first time that .... been to England

5 Are you still reading that guidebook?
   Haven't you .... reading that guidebook yet?

Speaking

▶ Part 2

1   Read the following task.

> You are on holiday and you are looking for a present for a friend of your own age. Talk together about the different souvenirs and decide which one would be the best.

2   First, think about the following questions on your own.

Which things might be expensive?

Which things need to be the correct size?

Which things are special products of this region?

Which things are useful?

Which things do you think he/she has already got?

Which things are unusual or original?

3   It is important to find out what your partner thinks. Here are three useful phrases for this. Write the words out in the correct order.

> *agree you do?*

> *you about how?*

> *you what think do?*

4   Now talk about the different things in the pictures and decide which one would be best.

Hot tip!

Don't immediately agree with one another or you'll have nothing to talk about. Discuss the advantages and disadvantages of each one before you finally decide.

Reading

▶ Part 2

1

- The people below are all visiting New Zealand.
- Here are descriptions of eight things to do in New Zealand.
- Decide which activity (**letters A–H**) would be the most suitable for each person or family (**numbers 1–5**).

> ### *Hot tip!*
>
> If you can't find an answer, go back and check through all the descriptions again, even those you have already chosen. You may have made a mistake earlier on.

HINT: *In the descriptions below there are some unusual words which are the names of places in New Zealand, e.g. the **Tutukaka** islands. You can recognise them because they begin with capital letters. Don't waste time looking them up in your dictionary!*

1

It is the end of Helen's holiday and she is looking for some presents to take back to her family in England. She does not have enough time for any other sightseeing or activities.

2

Mr and Mrs Reynolds would like to learn about the old ways of life in the New Zealand countryside. They have three young children who like animals very much.

3

Paul and Sally have just arrived in Auckland. They want to go out for lunch somewhere unusual, and to see the city at the same time.

4

Clara and Philip Holmes are interested in finding out more about New Zealand's past, especially the traditional food and entertainment.

5

Jackie wants to do something exciting while she is in New Zealand. She doesn't like heights but she likes water sports and is interested in birds, animals and fish.

A The Tutukaka islands, just off the coast of New Zealand, are one of the top ten best places for scuba diving in the world. Swim in the warm seas among friendly colourful fish, and explore underwater caves and tunnels with our qualified diving instructors. Suitable for everyone from beginners to experienced divers.

B Take a lift to the top of Sky Tower, Auckland's highest building, for fantastic views – and photos – of the city. There are three platforms from where you can see all over Auckland, and the restaurant at the top is the perfect place for a special meal!

C For the experience of a life-time, do a bungee jump at the Kawarau River. Safely tied to a strong rope, you jump from the bridge and fall 43 metres head-first to the river, touching the water before being pulled to safety. As a souvenir, you can buy the video of your jump, and of course, you must have the T-shirt!

D Go back in time and learn about the amazing history of New Zealand in the Te Papa Time Travel Experience. You can even see the birth of our country 65 million years ago! Lots of fun for children and adults too!

E Step into the magic world of adventure at Auckland Zoo. Just minutes from the City Centre, the zoo is home to over 600 animals. You can see monkeys, elephants and lions, as well as the famous kiwi, New Zealand's national bird.

F Rainbow Farm Show is a 'hands-on' experience that takes you through New Zealand's farming history, from sheep farming to the milk and wool industries – all in just 50 minutes! And as well as this, you can bottle-feed baby lambs, make cream or butter in the traditional way, or even ride a bull!

G The Maori people lived in New Zealand for hundreds of years before the Europeans arrived. In the Living Maori Village Experience you can enjoy an evening of traditional songs, dances and stories and eat foods cooked in the old Maori way on hot stones.

H You'll find a warm welcome at Victoria Market, with shops and stalls offering all kinds of souvenirs made from local products such as wood and stone, as well as a selection of international food and snacks. Right in the heart of Auckland, Victoria Market is the very best in affordable entertainment.

2 **Writing: postcard**

Imagine you are on holiday in New Zealand. Write a postcard to a friend. In your postcard, you should:

- say where you are
- describe something you have done
- explain what you plan to do next.

Write 35–45 words.

Reading

▶ **Part 5**

1 Read through the text quickly and choose the best way to complete this sentence.

The writer wrote this text to

a) warn travellers that it's important to wear the right clothing.

b) amuse readers by describing a woman who had an unusual life.

c) describe what life was like for women in 1892.

2 Now read the text again and choose the correct word for each space – **A**, **B**, **C** or **D**.

Remember! *You should always read the whole text through **before** you try to fill in any of the missing words.*

> **Hot tip!**
>
> Try to think what the word is **before** you look at the choices. This will make it easier to choose and you won't be confused by the other words.

The use of a good thick skirt

Mary Kingsley was born (0) ....*in*........... 1862 and lived a very quiet (1) .... with her parents in London (2) .... she was 31. Then she suddenly and unexpectedly (3) .... to become an explorer. She went to West Africa, (4) .... on foot and by boat through thick forests and along dangerous (5) .... She always wore a long wool skirt and carried an umbrella. One day she was walking along a path when she fell into a deep hole that people had (6) .... to catch wild animals. She (7) .... on sharp sticks at the bottom of the hole. This could have (8) .... her badly, but her clothes saved her. She said, 'It is at these times that you (9) .... the use of a good thick skirt.'

She made several more journeys, and wrote best-selling books about her (10) .... and the land and customs of the West African people.

0	A in	B on	C at	D to
1	A time	B life	C way	D place
2	A before	B when	C after	D until
3	A decided	B thought	C organised	D considered
4	A walking	B travelling	C being	D riding
5	A places	B lakes	C rivers	D waterfalls
6	A dug	B built	C placed	D set
7	A placed	B avoided	C found	D landed
8	A broken	B damaged	C spoiled	D hurt
9	A regret	B realise	C revise	D reserve
10	A advances	B escapes	C dangers	D adventures

3   Read through the text again and complete this sentence.

When she fell into the hole, Mary Kingsley was not injured because …

4   Can you think of other activities where people need special clothing? Match the activities 1–6 to the clothing that people wear and the reason they need it.

1 Skiers		a uniform		normal shoes would hurt.
2 Hikers		overalls		they need to look smart.
3 Mechanics		formal clothes		they might fall in the snow.
4 Police officers	wear	space suits	because	their clothes might get dirty.
5 Space explorers		boots		they need to have air to breathe.
6 Business executives		waterproof clothes		people need to recognise them.

Writing

▶ **Part 3: story**

> ### About the exam
>
> - You can choose to write a short story (about 100 words).
> - You might be given a title or the first line of the story.
>
> ### How to do it
>
> We use the past tense to tell stories. Usually the character or characters have a problem of some sort during the story. We read the story to find out how they solve the problem.
>
> 1 Read the question carefully.
> 2 Decide what will happen at the beginning, the middle and the end of your story.
> 3 Write your story.
> 4 Check your work.

1   Read the questions in the beginning and middle boxes and find the answers in the story below.

> **Beginning**
> - Where/When did the story begin?
> - What happened first?

> **Middle**
> - What was the problem?

> **End**
> - How was the problem solved?

One day last holidays I decided to go exploring on my own in the mountains. The time passed quickly and by late afternoon I was getting tired and hungry. 'Maybe I'll find a village soon,' I thought. But there was nothing. As it started to get dark, I realised I was completely lost. I could easily die, I thought, on this cold mountain. Suddenly …

2   The most important part of your story is the ending. Read the three different endings below and choose the best one. Why are the other two endings not so good?

A

... I found my mobile phone. I phoned my friends and told them about the problem. So they told the police and the police came onto the mountain and found me quickly and took me home in a police car.

B

... I saw a small house. I walked up to it. There was a man there. He was very nice and he said I could stay there. I was very glad, and I went in there and stayed the night. The next day I went home.

C

... a strange blue light appeared. It started to move and I followed it down the mountain until I was on the road home. Then it disappeared. I never found out what it was, but I think it saved my life.

3   Now write a story of your own, which starts with the sentence:

Last weekend I decided to go out on my own for the day.

Remember to think about the beginning, the middle and especially the end. When you have finished, check your work.

- Have you written complete sentences with capital letters and full stops?

- Have you used the past tense?

- Have you checked the spelling of difficult words?

Reading

▶ Part 1

1   Look at the texts in Exercise 2. Where might you see each one? Choose your answer from the list below.

a) in a hotel
b) in a transport office
c) at an airport
d) outside a night-club
e) in a holiday camp

2

- Look at the text in each question.
- What does it say?
- Mark the letter next to the correct explanation – **A**, **B** or **C**.

NO YOUNG PEOPLE UNDER 18 ALLOWED IN

1 A Only people over 18 can go in.
   B Anyone under 18 can go in.
   C Only young people should go in.

PLEASE LEAVE YOUR KEY AT RECEPTION BEFORE DEPARTURE

2 A Do not take your key with you when you leave.
   B Tell the receptionist when you want your key.
   C You can find your key at reception.

PLEASE SIGN UP FOR ALL ACTIVITIES BEFORE 9.30 AM

3 A All activities start before 9.30.
   B You should register for activities no later than 9.30.
   C Some activities start after 9.30.

Vocabulary

1 Tick (✓) the things you have in your classroom.

bags   blackboard   blinds   bookshelves
chairs   computer   cupboard   curtains
desks   notebooks   pictures   tables
video   whiteboard

2 Match the words in the box to the pictures below.

author   CDs   glue   highlighters
keyboard   mouse   pages   pencils
pens   rubber   ruler   screen
scissors   title

computer

book

pencil case

3

1 🖭 Listen to people talking about how they like to study. Complete the sentences below.

Susan likes studying with a ...

Keith likes studying with a ...

Pat likes studying with a ...

2 Complete the sentences below with your own ideas.

I like studying with a ... because ...

I don't like studying with a ... because ...

Reading

▶ **Part 4**

1

- Read the text and questions below.
- For each question, mark the letter next to the correct answer – **A**, **B**, **C** or **D**.

Maria's story

Mum and I came to London from the Philippines when I was ten. I loved my life and friends in London. The only thing I didn't like was our flat – it was noisy, and it only had one room. When I was 13, Mum decided to move to the north of England. My friends had a goodbye party for me. It was lovely but I cried because I was worried about starting again in a new school. I've still got the pencil case they gave me as a leaving present.

When we arrived at our new house in the country, I couldn't believe how much space there was. I've got my own bedroom and I've painted it blue – my favourite colour. School was difficult at first because some girls were horrible to me. I couldn't understand why, and I felt sad and lonely. But I've made some good friends now and I just don't talk to the others.

I've grown to like the north. I love the peaceful, wide open spaces and beautiful countryside. I sometimes miss London, but then I talk to Mum and she helps me see things aren't so bad. My advice to anyone who has to leave their friends is not to worry too much. You might even start liking your new home. I did.

1 What is the writer doing in this text?
   A comparing two different schools
   B explaining what makes a good friend
   C warning people about problems at school
   D describing a difficult situation
HINT: *Which is the main idea of the text?*

2 What can a reader find out from this text?
   A how to study at a school in the country
   B how country schools are different from town schools
   C the good things about living in the north
   D ways of staying in contact with friends

HINT: *The text only gives information about one of these.*

3 What does the writer think?
   A Teachers should look after new students.
   B It's good to share your problems with your mother.
   C New friends are never as good as the old ones.
   D People in London are very friendly.

HINT: *Here you need to find a statement that Maria would agree with, according to information she gives in the text.*

4 Why does the writer talk about her new bedroom?
   A to show an advantage of her new life
   B to show why some girls are jealous
   C to show how lonely she is
   D to show how kind her mother is

HINT: *Look at the first two sentences in paragraph 2.*

5 What would be a good title for the text?

   A **THE PARTY WHERE I CRIED**

   B **WHY I MISS LONDON**

   C **CHANGE CAN BE A GOOD THING**

   D **WHY IT'S GOOD TO MOVE SCHOOLS**

HINT: *Remember the title should summarise the main idea of the whole text.*

2 Would you like to move to a different country, or to a different part of your country? Why/Why not?

3 Writing: email

Imagine you have changed schools. Write an email to an English friend. In your email, you should:

• explain why you changed schools

• say what you miss about the old school

• say what you like about the new school.

Write 35–45 words.

Grammar

Obligation and prohibition; talking about rules and regulations

Rules

We have to wear a red top with the school badge on. And we've got to wear a red skirt too.

School rules
▶ All students **must** wear uniform.

We can talk about rules and obligations in three ways.

1 *They have to wear uniform.*

This is the most common way to talk about obligation.

2 *They've got to wear uniform.*

This is also quite common but is more informal.

3 *They must wear uniform.*

This is less common. It is often more formal.

1 Complete the sentences. Write one word in each gap.

1 Tim's .... wear brown trousers at school.

2 As well as that, he .... wear a white shirt and a brown tie.

3 There's also a rule that all the boys .... wear brown jackets and brown shoes.

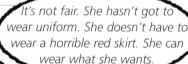

Negative rules, no rules

For rules about things we **can't** do, we can say *mustn't, can't* or *aren't allowed to*.

When we talk about things that we can choose **not** to do, we can say *don't have to* or *haven't got to*.

It's not fair. She hasn't got to wear uniform. She doesn't have to wear a horrible red skirt. She can wear what she wants.

You mustn't wear jewellery at school. You can't wear high-heeled shoes.

2   Think about your school. Which of these statements are true for you?

1 We have to wear uniform.

2 The boys have got to wear ties.

3 We can't wear jeans.

4 The girls don't have to wear skirts – they can wear trousers if they want to.

5 We have to wear clothes of a certain colour.

6 We don't have to wear any special clothes – we're allowed to wear anything we like.

7 In my primary school we had to wear a uniform.

8 We didn't have to wear special clothes in my primary school.

3   Writing, Part 1

Here are some sentences about school life. For each question, complete the second sentence so that it means the same as the first. Use no more than three words.

1 In my school the students can choose what they want to wear – there's no uniform.

In my school we don't .... to wear uniform.

2 Our teacher said we must give in our homework.

Our teacher said we .... give in our homework.

3 Have we got to write a story?

Do .... to write a story?

4 You know you mustn't leave before 3.30.

You know you .... allowed to leave before 3.30.

5 He was told not to miss the class.

He's .... to go to the class.

Reading

▶ **Part 5**

1   Read the following text. Don't forget to read the title. Don't fill in any spaces yet. What is the main purpose of the text?

a) to advertise a course for children in England

b) to describe a typical school day in England

c) to give information about education in England

2   Now read the text again and choose the correct word for each space – **A, B, C** or **D**.

English Schools

In England, most children (**0**) ...*attend*........ state schools, although about 12% are educated privately. All children start primary school (**1**) .... they are five years old. At the age of 11 they move on to a secondary school, and they (**2**) .... to stay there until they are 16. At this age they are (**3**) .... to leave school and look for a job. (**4**) ...., many stay at school until they are 18 and then go on to further education.

The (**5**) .... year begins in September and ends in July, and is divided into three terms. Students have a holiday at Christmas and Easter as well as a long (**6**) .... in the summer. The day normally (**7**) .... from 9.00 am to about 4.00 pm, and the pupils usually (**8**) .... their lunch at school. Most schools (**9**) .... a hot meal, but some students bring sandwiches instead. There are often (**10**) .... after school, such as sports, drama clubs and music.

0	A attend	B go	C follow	D get
1	A until	B as	C when	D so
2	A will	B must	C can	D have
3	A sent	B ruled	C made	D allowed
4	A However	B Although	C Then	D But
5	A school	B study	C learning	D teaching
6	A space	B interval	C pause	D break
7	A studies	B runs	C goes	D works
8	A take	B do	C make	D eat
9	A pay	B bring	C provide	D present
10	A activities	B games	C plays	D hobbies

3   Read the text again and complete the sentences below.

1 In my country education is different because we ... but in England they ...

2 In my country education is similar because we both ...

Writing

▶ Part 3: letter

1   Find three punctuation mistakes and four grammar mistakes in the sentences below. Underline the mistakes and then correct them.

In my school there is thirty pupils in each class. We dont have lunch in school because the school day finish at lunchtime. every afternoon we do homework or sometimes I am playing football with my friends I think we have too many homework to do every day.

....

....

....

....

....

2   Match the sentence halves and choose a different connecting word for each one.

1 My school is quite big and modern	but	we don't have to pay to attend classes.
2 It is a state school	and	we can stay until we are 18.
3 We can do sport after school if we want to	or	it has about 1,000 students.
4 We can either leave school at 16	so	we don't have to – so I don't!

3   Do the following task. To help you with ideas, look back at the information in Reading, Part 5.

TASK

● This is part of a letter you receive from your English friend, Katy.

I'm really looking forward to staying with your family and going to school with you. What is your school like?

● Now write a letter to Katy, telling her about your school and what you do there. Write about 100 words.

Dear Katy,
I'm really glad you're coming to stay and I hope you'll enjoy coming to school with me...

Speaking

▶ **Part 2**

You have a new teacher and she wants to know which ways of studying you find most enjoyable. Talk together about these ways of studying, and decide which ones you would like to use.

▶ **Part 3**

1

1 When you describe the photograph in Part 3 of the exam, you have to talk about what you can actually see, and also make suggestions about why the people are there and how they are feeling. Look at picture A. Which of the following things can you actually see in the picture? Write six sentences about the picture.

table   books   lamp   pen   bookcase
papers   desk   chair   posters

Example:
There's a girl sitting on a bed.
The girl is ...
I can see ...
There's a ...
There are ...

> **Hot tip!**
>
> When we are not sure about something we often use *might* or *could*.
>
> *She might/could be there because it's quiet.*
> *She might/could be feeling tired.*

2 Why might the person choose to study there? Think about the advantages and disadvantages of being there.

3 How might she be feeling?

4   Now listen to a student describing what he can see in the picture and complete the sentences below.

I .... a girl sitting on a bed. She's .... She's in her bedroom. I can see a .... next to the bed and some .... on the wall. There are .... on the bed

Maybe she likes studying there because it's ...., and she's got everything she needs. One problem might be that it's a bit too ....

She might be feeling .... and maybe she'd like to .... Or she could be feeling quite ....

2   Now look at picture B. Talk about:

• what you can see in the picture
• why the person is there
• how they might be feeling.

> **Hot tip!**
>
> When you talk about the picture, it is a good idea to use these three points to give you ideas to talk about. There will always be people in your picture.

▶ **Part 4**

Work with a partner. Talk together about the places where you like to study and the places where you don't like to study. You can use these ideas to help you.

• places at school
• places at home
• other buildings
• studying outside

> **Hot tip!**
>
> The discussion in Part 4 is always connected to the topic of both the photographs in Part 3. The examiner will take your photograph away when you have finished speaking about it, but you can use ideas from the photographs to start your conversation in Part 4 if you want. However, you should also add more thoughts of your own as well. Remember to give reasons for your ideas.

3   **Writing: note**

You want to study with your friend. Write a note to your friend. In your note, you should:

• tell your friend where to meet you
• suggest a time to meet
• explain what you want to study.

Write 35–45 words.

Reading

▶ Part 1

- Look at the text in each question.
- What does it say?
- Mark the letter next to the correct explanation – **A**, **B** or **C**.

> Last entry to
> the museum
> 1 hour before
> closing time

1   A   You can enter the museum half an hour before it closes.
    B   You can stay in the museum for one hour only.
    C   You can't enter the museum during the hour before it closes.

> **Show this
> advertisement
> to get 10%
> discount on
> entrance to the
> museum**

2   A   You must show the advertisement to get into the museum.
    B   You pay less at the museum if you show the advertisement.
    C   Entry to the museum is described in the advertisement.

Listening

▶ Part 4

1   Look through the statements below and think about these questions.

a) Who is having driving lessons?

b) Do you think this person is happy or unhappy about the situation?

		A YES	B NO
1	Jim was hurt in a car accident when he was young.	☐	☐
2	Jim's driving teacher says Jim is no good at driving.	☐	☐
3	Kate thought her driving teacher was good.	☐	☐
4	Jim thinks he needs quite a lot more driving lessons.	☐	☐
5	Jim is worried about Kate giving him lessons.	☐	☐
6	Kate is going to speak to Jim's driving teacher.	☐	☐

2   📼 Now do the task.

- Look at the six statements above.
- You will hear a conversation between two teenagers, a boy, Jim, and a girl, Kate.
- Decide if you think each statement is correct or incorrect.
- If you think it is correct, put a tick (✓) in the box under **A** for **YES**. If you think it is not correct, put a tick (✓) in the box under **B** for **NO**.

3   Who would be the best driving teacher for you? Why?

1   someone in your family
2   a friend
3   a driving instructor

What's it like outside?

Vocabulary

1 🖭 Listen and complete the picture below.

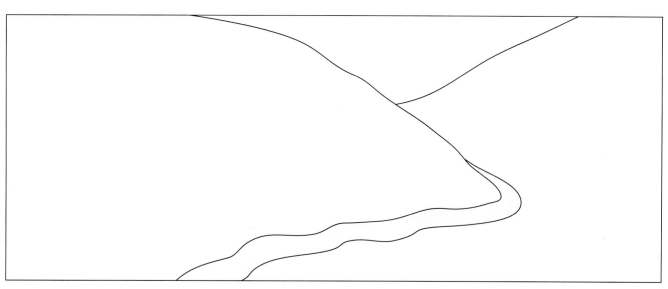

2 Choose the best word to complete these sentences.

1 If you go to Scotland, you will see some beautiful
   ....
   A scenery   B nature

2 We're planning to go on a .... of the
   Welsh mountains next year.
   A trip   B tour

3 Please .... me to take my boots when I go
   on my walking holiday.
   A remember   B remind

4 In my ...., the government should look
   after the countryside and keep it tidy.
   A idea   B opinion

5 After all the rain, the .... was very wet
   under my feet when I went for a walk.
   A ground   B floor

6 He was lost on the mountain all night, but luckily he
   was .... warm clothes, so he was all right.
   A putting on   B wearing

3 🖭 Listen to people talking about where they live, and complete these sentences.

1 Susie lives in the ....
   She lives in an .... with a
   ....
   She likes it because the people are ....
   .... and she can go ....
   She doesn't want to live in ....
   because it's .... and
   ....

2 James lives in the ....
   He lives in a ....
   He likes being near the ....
   and ....
   He doesn't want to live in the ....
   because it's ....

Reading

▶ Part 2

1

- The people below all want to do something in the country.
- There are descriptions opposite of eight things to do.
- Decide which activity (**letters A–H**) would be the most suitable for each person or group (**numbers 1–5**).

Remember! *You cannot use the same activity for more than one person or group.*

1  Emmy is six years old and lives in a town. She's frightened of animals. Her grandmother thinks touching small animals would make her more confident.

2  Ann and Colin are spending the afternoon with their father, who wants to do something outside, but isn't interested in history. They hate walking and like speed and excitement. Colin doesn't like animals.

3  The Williams family would like to spend the day together walking in the open air, and they want to see something exciting. They're interested in nature.

4  Jessica is 14. She lives in London, but she loves animals, especially horses. She hasn't actually done any riding yet, but she's keen to try.

5  Mike and Janet are interested in history and nature. They quite like walking and want to get some exercise, but the weather forecast isn't very good today and they don't want to get wet.

A Black Hole Caves

These amazing caves were discovered in 1858 by a local farmer. The two-hour guided tour includes the 'dining room' cave with its table and chairs of natural rock, and ends with a boat trip along an underwater river. An experience not to be missed!

B Happy Rest

At Happy Rest we care for horses who have not been looked after by their owners. We offer them a comfortable home where they can end their days peacefully. Visitors can meet the horses, and learn about our work in our information centre. Guided tours available.

C Castle Hill, Denton

If you are in the small village of Denton, it's worth paying a visit to Castle Hill. Only a few stones remain of the original 12th-century castle, but the area is full of beautiful wild flowers, and is ideal for a quiet picnic.

D Creston

There's nothing quite like a trip to Creston. Take a train ride back in time and experience all the sights and sounds of the golden age of steam trains. Then visit our indoor garden centre where you can buy unusual plants for the house and garden.

E African Adventure

Experience the excitement of your very own African adventure. Follow explorer paths through woods, past lakes and over hills to meet some of Africa's wild animals including lions, zebras and giraffes. You'll need a whole day to do the walk – but it's worth it!

F Staintondale Horses

Horse and pony lovers, this is the place for you! See our traditional farm horses working in their natural surroundings. Go for a ride on country paths with experienced trainers on our well-behaved horses. Picnic area, café and souvenir shop.

G Duckling Farm

There's always plenty to do on Duckling Farm, where everyone can get to know our friendly farm animals. Feed the cows and sheep you meet along the way. Hold a baby rabbit and feed the lambs and piglets from a bottle. Our helpful farm staff will make sure that even the youngest visitor has a good time!

H Quad trekking

Quad bikes are like motorbikes, but their four strong wheels make them easier to ride and much more fun! Even if you've never driven before, our qualified instructors will train you in just a few minutes and you can then experience the fun of riding over woodland paths at up to 50 kph.

---

2   Which of the activities above would you like to do:

- with your family?
- with your friends?

Speaking

▶ Part 2

1   Read the following task.

> You are going out to the country for a day with your friend. Talk together about the different things you could do and then decide which one to choose.

2

1 Laura and Mike are discussing the first three pictures. Fill in the spaces with phrases from the box.

a) actually I'd rather
b) ..., are they?
c) Don't you think so?
d) How about
e) how do you feel about
f) I think it would be nice.
g) I'm not all that keen on it.
h) I'd like to
i) That's true.
j) Well, I'm not sure.

Laura   (1) .... go horse-riding. I've never done it and I've always wanted to try. Can you ride?

Mike   I've never tried, but (2) .... It looks quite difficult – and it's a long way to fall. You could hurt yourself quite badly. (3) ....

Laura   Well, I'm not sure. But all right – if you don't want to do that, (4) .... walking? That's not dangerous.

Mike   (5) .... And it's good exercise – it's supposed to be really good for you. But don't you need special boots if you're walking far? I've only got these shoes, and they're not really strong enough, (6) ....

Laura   No. Well, you could borrow my brother's boots. I think he's got some.

Mike   I don't know if that would work. I've got really big feet. They might not be very comfortable. (7) .... just going for a picnic? We could put some food in the car and find a nice place.

Laura   (8) .... You mean just drive around in the car and then sit and eat?

Mike   Yes. (9) .... We could just relax.

Laura   But (10) .... get some exercise.

Mike   Oh, OK.

2   ▣ Now listen and compare your answers with the recording.

3   Cover up the dialogue in Exercise 2 and do the whole speaking task in Exercise 1 with a partner.

Listening

▶ **Part 4**

1 📼

- Look at the six statements.
- You will hear a conversation between a female student, Jane, and a male student, Neil, who have been to see a film.
- Decide if you think each statement is correct or incorrect.
- If you think it is correct, put a tick (✓) in the box under **A** for **YES**. If you think it is not correct, put a tick (✓) in the box under **B** for **NO**.

Remember! *Underline the names of the people in the statements when you read them through.*

		A YES	B NO
1	They both liked the last part of the film.	☐	☐
2	Neil thinks the storm scene was like a real storm.	☐	☐
3	Neil says the first part of the film was easy to understand.	☐	☐
4	Jane thinks the fishermen were interesting people.	☐	☐
5	Neil thinks the fishermen were partly to blame.	☐	☐
6	The weather forecast said there would be rain today.	☐	☐

2 Have you seen a film recently where the weather played a part in the story? Tell your partner about it. Discuss the answer to these questions.

What sort of weather was it?

How did it affect the story?

What happened in the end?

Writing

▶ **Part 3: story**

1 Read this writing task.

> **TASK**
>
> Write a story beginning:
> *The weather forecast said it was going to be a bright, sunny day.*
> Use about 100 words.

2 Write your story. It will probably involve a situation where there is a sudden change in the weather which causes problems.

Think about where your story is set, e.g. the sea, a river or lake, a mountain or valley.

Who were the people? (yourself, or other people)

What was the problem?

What happened in the end?

It will help you to write notes on your ideas and use these as a plan for your story. Write short answers to the questions above and use these as your notes. For example,

the sea

me and my friend

a storm came and the boat sank

we escaped

frightened of the sea after that

Now complete the story, using the first line given in the task. Add extra details to your notes, such as how you felt at the start, what you did and how you felt at the end. Join the sentences together using linking words such as *then* and *after that*. Try to make the ending interesting or dramatic!

Remember! *Check your work for spelling, grammar and punctuation at the end.*

> *Hot tip!*
>
> You probably won't have time to write your story out twice. Leave plenty of room on your paper so that you can write corrections above any mistakes. It doesn't matter if you have lots of corrections as long as your work can be read easily.

Reading

▶ Part 5

1 Look at the title and read through the text quickly. Don't fill in any spaces yet. What is the text about?

a) why the weather forecast is often wrong

b) the effect of the weather on people's lives

c) what the weather is like in different countries

2

- Read the text and choose the correct word for each space.
- For each question, mark the letter next to the correct word – **A**, **B**, **C** or **D**.

> **Hot tip!**
>
> Always read the title of the text as this will give you an idea of what it is about.

The weather

Rain, clouds, sunshine, wind – what (0) ...*causes*..... them? And why are they important to us? The weather influences farming, fishing and every part of our daily life, and so we (1) .... to know in advance (2) .... it will be like. Weather forecasters try to (3) .... us with details of weather conditions for at (4) .... 24 hours ahead, and often for up to a week. To do this they depend (5) .... thousands of separate (6) .... of information about the weather, which are (7) .... from all over the world. But the weather not only changes what people do every day, it can (8) .... change the way they feel. (9) .... example, the warm, dusty wind of the Mediterranean is famous for (10) .... people feel annoyed. And it's true that we all feel better when it's sunny rather than when it's raining!

3 How has the weather affected you and your family in the last week? Tell your partner about it.

4 Writing: email

You have arranged to have a picnic with some friends tomorrow, but the weather forecast is very bad. Write an email to your friends. In your email, you should:

- explain the problem
- suggest something different to do
- arrange a meeting place.

Write 35–45 words.

0	A causes	B does	C goes	D gets
1	A must	B can	C should	D need
2	A how	B what	C where	D when
3	A give	B show	C provide	D tell
4	A last	B once	C least	D first
5	A on	B with	C at	D from
6	A pieces	B words	C numbers	D facts
7	A made	B moved	C told	D collected
8	A again	B also	C too	D so
9	A As	B In	C For	D By
10	A making	B having	C seeing	D doing

Grammar

Direct and reported speech

When we write what someone has said, we can do it in two ways.

Direct speech

She said, 'I like walking, but I don't want to go for a walk today.'

'I saw Tom this morning,' he said.

Here we write the exact words that were spoken, with inverted commas ('speech marks') around them. The reporting verb, e.g. *(she) said*, can come at the beginning or at the end.

Reported speech

*She said (that) **she liked** walking, but **she didn't want to go for a walk that day**.*

*He said (that) **he had seen Tom that morning**.*

With reported speech there are often changes in:

- the pronouns (e.g. *I → she/he*)
- the tense (e.g. *like → liked*; *don't want → didn't want*; *saw → had seen*)
- expressions of time (e.g. *today → that day*; *this morning → that morning*)
- expressions of place (e.g. *here → there*)

1 Match the sentences which have the same meaning, and underline the words that have changed.

1 'I hope to see you today,' she said.	a) She said that she was going to see them the next day.
2 She said, 'I am going to see you tomorrow.'	b) She said that she had stayed in a lovely hotel quite near there.
3 'I was on holiday last week,' she said.	c) She said that she hoped to see them that day.
4 She said, 'I stayed in a lovely hotel quite near here.'	d) She said that she had been on holiday the week before.

Reported speech with questions and commands

When we write a question, we can also use direct or indirect speech.

'Are you coming?' he asked. → He asked if she was coming.

'When did they arrive?' he asked her. → He asked her when they had arrived.

Notice the change in word order. In direct questions, the subject and verb change places. In indirect questions, they don't.

When we write a command, we use the imperative form for direct speech, and the infinitive with *to* for reported speech.

'Stop talking!' he ordered them. → He ordered them to stop talking.

'Don't move!' he said. → He told them not to move.

2 Match the pairs of sentences and fill in the missing words.

1 'Do you want a sandwich?' I asked.	a) I asked .... I .... have a holiday.
2 'Go away now!' we said to him.	b) She .... the children .... be quiet.
3 'Can I have a holiday?' I asked.	c) We told him .... go away immediately.
4 'Don't touch it!' he ordered me.	d) She asked when .... see me.
5 'Be quiet!' she said to the children.	e) I asked him if he .... a sandwich.
6 'When can I see you?' she asked.	f) He told .... to touch it.

3   Punctuate these sentences. You may need to add capital letters, full stops, commas, speech marks, question marks and exclamation marks (!).

1   she said I am hoping to arrive in the evening

2   where do you live she asked

3   I never expected to see you here he said

4   why not she asked

5   stop here he ordered them

6   they said they had had a long journey

4   **Writing, Part 1**

Here are some sentences about a picnic. For each question, complete the second sentence so that it means the same as the first. Use no more than three words.

1   They said they wanted to go on a picnic that afternoon.
They said 'We '............................ to go on a picnic this afternoon.'

2   They said that they had seen a nice place the day before.
They said, '............................ a nice place yesterday.'

3   Carlos asked if he could come with them.
Carlos said, '.................................... come with you?'

4   They told him not to worry about the weather.
They said, '........................ worry about the weather.'

5   They said they had already bought the food.
They said, '........................ already bought the food.'

Reading

▶ Part 1

- Look at the text in each question.
- What does it say?
- Mark the letter next to the correct explanation – **A, B** or **C**.

> Picnic area – no dogs or ball games please

1 A People can eat here but they can't play any games.
   B Dogs are not allowed in places where there are ball games.
   C People can't bring dogs here or play with balls.

> **Please do not pick the flowers growing wild in the forest**

2 A You mustn't pick any wild flowers in the forest.
   B You shouldn't take the flowers that have been picked.
   C You can't go into the forest where the wild flowers are growing.

A day's work

Vocabulary

1 Would you rather be a journalist or the manager of a company? Which job:

- has the most responsibility?
- has the longest hours?
- has the best pay?
- is the most useful to other people?
- is the most enjoyable?

2 Find the hidden jobs in the jumbled letters below and fill in the gaps in each question. Then discuss the answer.

1

liopt   odotrc

Would you rather be a .... or a
...................? Why?

2

idks yojkce   etidnts

Would you rather be a .... or a
...................? Why?

3

ninegere   ahrrderisse

Would you rather be an .... or a
...................? Why?

4

esrycerat   sitcsneit

Would you rather be a .... or a
...................? Why?

5

refigrihetf   lpcoie friceof

Would you rather be a .... or a
...................? Why?

3   Correct the mistakes in the sentences below.

1 A firefighter looks after your teeth.
2 A pilot types letters and answers the telephone.
3 A doctor puts out fires.
4 An engineer makes sure people follow the law.
5 A police officer plays records in clubs and discos.
6 A dentist washes and cuts your hair.
7 A disk jockey does experiments in a laboratory.
8 A scientist looks after people's health.
9 A hairdresser builds bridges or repairs machinery.
10 A secretary flies planes.

4   Complete the sentences by adding the correct ending to the word.

Example:

I'm a pil.ot...... and I mainly do international flights.

1 She's a reception.......... in a hotel.
2 She's a nurse who works with patien.......... in the local hospital.
3 He's a sports instruct.......... at the leisure centre.
4 He's an assist.......... in a department store.
5 Since she's had the children she's been a full-time house.......... .
6 He's a policeman and he sometimes has to arrest crim.......... .
7 Sherlock Holmes was a private detect.......... who solved many crimes.
8 My father's a business.......... and he has to do a lot of travelling.

Speaking

▶ **Part 3**

You are going to talk about a picture showing the different places in which people work. Work with a partner. Choose one picture each and describe it to your partner. Try to talk for one minute.

Remember! *Talk about:*
* *what you can see*
* *the people and why you think they are there*
* *how they might be feeling.*

▶ **Part 4**

One of the pictures above showed someone working outside. Work with a partner. Talk together about the things you like doing outside in the summer and in the winter. Try to talk for about three minutes.

Reading

▶ Part 5

1   Look at the title and read the text below. Don't fill in the spaces yet. What is the text about?

a) a girl with a wonderful voice

b) music for the Queen

c) travelling round the world

2   Now read the text again and choose the correct word for each space – **A**, **B**, **C** or **D**.

Charlotte Church ▪ ▪ ▪

▪ Charlotte Church (**0**) ....*was*...... born in a small town

▪ in Wales in 1986 and has loved music all her life. At nine

years old, she started to (**1**) .... singing lessons.

Soon afterwards she sang on a television programme

for children, and was an immediate success.

(**2**) .... then her records have sold more than

7 million (**3**) .... She has sung for the Queen

and for Prince Charles, and has (**4**) .... the

President of the USA and the Pope.

In (**5**) .... of being famous, she still wants to

live the life (**6**) .... a typical teenager. Like

(**7**) .... other girl she enjoys shopping and

playing computer (**8**) .... When she is not

travelling round the world, she (**9**) .... a local

all-girls school. 'My friends are all really great,' she says.

'There's (**10**) .... jealousy at all.'

0	A was	B is	C has	D did
1	A go	B learn	C take	D study
2	A After	B Following	C Since	D For
3	A copies	B ones	C numbers	D parts
4	A known	B met	C played	D performed
5	A place	B spite	C case	D way
6	A of	B as	C for	D with
7	A all	B most	C any	D the
8	A programmes	B sports	C activities	D games
9	A goes	B studies	C visits	D attends
10	A not	B no	C none	D never

Language spot

*Charlotte still wants **to live** the life of a normal teenager.*

*She enjoys **shopping**.*

When we have two verbs together, the second one can be either the infinitive (*to live*) or an *-ing* form (*shopping*).

a) Underline the correct form in these sentences. Use a dictionary if you want to.

   1 I want *working/to work* in the entertainment industry.

   2 I enjoy *performing/to perform* in public.

   3 When I've finished *studying/to study* at school, I'll do a drama course.

   4 I hope *being/to be* famous one day.

   5 I expect *making/to make* a lot of money.

   6 But I'll refuse *letting/to let* my success affect me.

b) Complete this table with verbs from the sentences above.

Verbs followed by *-ing*	Verbs followed by infinitive
....	....
....	....
....	....
....	....

c) Complete these sentences with your own ideas.

   1 My little sister keeps ... – I hate it!

   2 I try to avoid ...

   3 I recently decided ... because ...

   4 After trying very hard, I managed ... and I felt really pleased.

d) Now add these verbs to the table above.

Reading

▶ Part 3

1 Look at the pictures. Do you own anything made in this way? Can anyone in your family do any of these things?

1 lace-making

2 embroidery

3 knitting

4 woodcarving

2

- Look at the sentences below about a museum.
- Read the text to decide if each sentence is correct or incorrect.
- If it is correct, mark **A**.
- If it not correct, mark **B**.

Remember! *The statements always come in the same order as the information in the text.*

1 Lace has been made in Middleton for almost 200 years.

2 Most lace factories were in nearby villages.

3 Children used to work in Middleton's lace factories.

4 The lace-making machines are over 150 years old.

5 The Lace Market is inside the museum.

6 There is a good choice of lace for sale in the shop.

7 Some lace goods have to be specially ordered by customers.

8 Teachers can bring groups of children to visit the museum.

9 The museum has its own car park.

10 There are special buses from the rail station to the museum.

Discover Middleton Lace at the Museum of Middleton Lace.

●

Learn about how lace is made.

●

Talk to people who have spent a lifetime making lace.

●

Buy Middleton Lace in our special shop.

The Story of Lace

Middleton is world famous for its beautiful lace. At the Museum of Middleton Lace you can see where the city's lace industry began nearly two centuries ago, listen to stories of what working life was like in the past and have the chance to talk to people who still work with the lace machines.

The museum shows the early days of lace production, when it was made by hand in the surrounding small villages. It follows the rapid growth of the industry during the 19th century, when large factories producing machine-made lace were built in Middleton, employing many young children. And you can see the latest computer technology that is available in the industry today.

We have two working machines that are operated daily by our three 'twisthands' (lace machine workers) who have over 150 years' experience between them.

The Lace Market

In addition to the museum we offer a tour of the historic Lace Market. Many people are surprised to learn that the Lace Market is not actually a market place, but is the name for a whole area of Middleton where there were a large number of warehouses used for storing the lace, as well as many lace salesrooms. By walking round the 'market' you can gain a real feeling of what the area would have been like when it was the most important lace centre in England.

The Shop

The Museum Shop has one of the largest selections of lace goods in the UK. Even more is available by special order. If you can't decide what to buy at the time, we also have a free mail-order catalogue. To ensure that you receive a copy, please make sure that you are on our mailing list.

The Lace Museum

You can walk around the museum at your own pace. The museum is suitable for young and old, male or female. It is ideal for school parties – children can come and discover more about Middleton's history, see the actual buildings where the lace was made, and handle lace. An educational pack is available for teachers.

The Museum of Middleton Lace is centrally located near major city centre car parks. It is convenient for city centre bus services and within walking distance of the rail station.

Listening

▶ **Part 3**

1

- Look at the notes about jobs for film actors.
- Some information is missing.
- You will hear someone talking on the radio about the jobs.
- For each question, fill in the missing information in the numbered space.

Remember! *Read through the notes first to get a general idea of the topic.*

Jobs for film actors

Film actors needed – experience not necessary

Film is a (1)... called *Victoria*!

50 young people needed to play
(2) ....

Must be aged 11–16 and less than
(3) ....
tall.

Small number of parts for boys who can
(4) ....

Needed for the first two weeks in
(5) ....

For more information go to
(6) ....
at 10.00 a.m. on Saturday.

2 Would you like to do a job like this in your holidays? Why/Why not? Think of three things you'd want to find out from the film company before you agreed to take the job.

Grammar

Using connecting words

> *Because, as, since*
>
> Phrases introduced by these words answer the question *Why?*
>
> The part of the sentence with the connecting word can come before or after the main part of the sentence.
>
> *Rita's looking for a job* **because/as/since** *she needs to save some money.*
>
> **Because/As/Since** *she needs to save some money, Rita's looking for a job.*

1 Match the beginnings and endings to make three more sentences about Rita. Underline the reason in each sentence.

1 Since she's still at school,   **a)** because the pay is quite good.

2 There are lots of restaurants in her town   **b)** she can only work at weekends.

3 She's going to look for a job as a waitress   **c)** as it's a tourist centre.

> *So that, in order to*
>
> Phrases introduced by these words tell us the purpose for doing something.
>
> *Rick is studying German and Spanish. He wants to work in the tourist industry.*
>
> *Rick is studying German and Spanish* **so that he can get** *a job in the tourist industry.* (so that + subject + verb)
>
> *Rick is studying German and Spanish* **in order to get** *a job in the tourist industry.* (in order + to-infinitive)

2 Join each of the sentence halves below in two different ways, as in the examples above.

1 He wants to work in tourism .... /
.... travel around the world.

2 He wants to travel around the world .... /
.... see how different people live.

Although, while

Although links two contrasting ideas.
It has a similar meaning to *but*.

It's raining but I'll go out anyway.

Although it's raining, I'll go out.

We put the idea we think is most important at the end of the sentence.

Maria Theresa's no good at English. She's very good at French.

Although Maria Theresa's no good at English, *she speaks good French.*

Maria Theresa speaks good French **although she's no good at English.**

While can be used in similar way, but must come at the beginning of the sentence.

While he finds the journey tiring, *he refuses to get the bus.*

3   Fill in the gaps using *but*, *although* or *while*.

1 .... / .... Mr Green doesn't like his job much, he does have a lot of friends there.

2 Mr Green doesn't like his job much .... / .... he does have a lot of friends there.

3 .... Peter is good at tennis, his brother is better than him at football.

4 His brother is better at football .... Peter always beats him at tennis.

So/such ... that

So/such ... that link information about the cause of something and the result in the same sentence.

My first job was very boring. As a result, I left.

My first job was **so boring that** *I left.*
(*so* + adjective + *that*)

It was **such boring work that** *I left.*
(*such* + adjective + uncountable noun)

It was **such a boring job that** *I left.* (*such* (+ article) + adjective + noun + *that*)

4   Rewrite each of these sentences twice, using first *so* and then *such*.

Example: The job was very interesting and because of this I loved it.

1 *The job was* <u>so</u> *interesting* <u>that</u> *I loved it.*

2 *It was* <u>such an</u> *interesting job* <u>that</u> *I loved it.*

1 The office was very cold, and as a result, I got ill.

2 The computers were very old and they were always breaking down.

3 The weather was very bad, and because of this I couldn't stay outside.

4 The day was very sunny, and this meant it was difficult to see my computer screen.

5   **Writing, Part 1**

Here are some sentences about a job. For each question, complete the second sentence so that it means the same as the first. Use no more than three words.

1 He learned to drive in order to get a job as a salesman.

He learnt to drive .... he could get a job as a salesman.

2 While the pay wasn't very good, the job was interesting.

The job was interesting, ... the pay wasn't very good.

3 He knew the work was important, so he did it very carefully.

He did the work very carefully .... he knew it was important.

4 It was a useful qualification and everyone wanted to get it.

It was .... qualification that everyone wanted to get it.

5 He travelled a lot and was hardly ever at home.

He did so .... that he was hardly ever at home.

Writing

▶ Part 3: letter

1 Read this writing task and look at the notes below.

TASK

● This is part of a letter you receive from your English penfriend.

I really can't decide what job I want to do. How about you? What sort of work would you like to do?

● Now write a letter to your penfriend telling him/her what sort of work you would like to do in the future.

● Write about 100 words.

Notes:
- job I'd like
- what the job would involve
- why I'd like it

2 Now do the task, using the notes to help you.

Hot tip!

Make sure you write about all the points mentioned in the task in your letter and remember to plan the information you will include before you begin to write.

Language spot

Remember you are writing about the future.

If you are sure that you will do your dream job, you can use future forms such as:
I'm going to be a teacher.
This suggests that you definitely intend to do this.

If you are less sure, you need to use a conditional form (see Unit 6).
If I pass all my exams, I'll go to university to study business.
If I could do any job in the world, I'd be a professional football player.

Reading

▶ Part 1

1 Signs in different places often use the same words. Complete the signs with words from the box below. You will need to use some words more than once.

allowed	please	in case	no
accept	must		

1 Dogs are not .... in the shop.
2 .... of fire, leave by the nearest exit.
3 .... do not take towels from your room to beach.
4 .... use other door until next week when reception re-opens.
5 Films rented on Friday .... be returned on Sunday.
6 We .... all types of credit cards in this shop.
7 Children under 15 are not .... to rent this film.
8 Smoking is not .... anywhere in the building.
9 .... parking – private road.
10 Private property. .... entry.

2 Where could you see the signs in 1–10 in Exercise 1? Write one number in each gap. (Some signs could be in more than one place.)

a) a shop or place where you rent videos:

....

b) an office or a hotel:

....

c) outside:

....

3 It may help you to understand the meaning of a sign or a note if you think about the words that have been left out. Match each sign in Exercise 1 to its meaning below and underline the words that are different.

a) <u>You must not smoke</u> anywhere in the building. ....8....

b) You can use all types of credit card in this shop. ....

c) You are not allowed to park your car at any time because the road is private property. ....

d) You can't rent this film if you are under 15. ....

e) You are not allowed to enter at any time because this is a private place. ....

f) You must use the other door until next week as reception is closed now. ....

g) If you rent a film on Friday then you have to return it on Sunday. ....

h) You should not take the towels from your room to the beach. ....

i) If there is a fire, you must leave using the nearest exit. ....

j) You must not bring dogs into the shop. ....

4 Match the signs below to the sentences. Write in the missing words.

1 Stand behind red line when waiting for service.

2 Apply for job on enclosed form.

3 For use in emergencies only.

4 Do not run in corridor.

5 Meet you at six. Don't be late!

a) You .... only use this in emergencies.

b) ..You.... ..must.. stand behind ..the.. red line when ...you.. ...are.. waiting for service.

c) .... meet you at six. You .... be late!

d) You .... apply for .... job on .... enclosed form.

e) You .... run in .... corridor.

5

• Look at the text in each question.

• What does it say?

• Mark the letter next to the correct explanation – **A**, **B** or **C**.

Closed until 9.30 on Wednesdays for staff training. Normal opening hours 9–5.30.

1 A Staff are trained on Wednesday mornings until 9.30.
   B Staff come to work at 9.30 on Wednesdays.
   C Staff open the shop at the normal time on Wednesdays.

Escalator to conference room out of order. Use the stairs opposite the reception desk.

2 A You can go to the conference room using the escalator.
   B You must use the stairs to go to reception.
   C You must take the stairs to the conference room.

Down town

Vocabulary

1 In the box there are the names of some places you can find in a town or city. How many can you find in five minutes? Use the pictures to help you.

T	O	W	E	R	B	L	O	C	K
R	T	Q	C	S	H	O	P	A	B
E	A	H	M	A	R	K	E	T	U
S	X	L	E	Z	F	X	B	H	S
T	I	I	D	A	O	E	A	E	S
A	R	B	B	I	T	Z	N	D	T
U	A	R	B	X	S	R	K	R	A
R	N	A	A	A	F	C	E	A	T
A	K	R	P	A	R	K	O	L	I
N	R	Y	C	I	N	E	M	A	O
T	H	O	S	P	I	T	A	L	N

2

1 Listen to a man describing the city where he lives and fill in the missing words.

In the middle of the city there's a square, and in the square there's a (1) .... On the north side of the square there's a (2) ...., and on the east side there's a (3) ...., with a shop next to it. Next to the (4) .... there's a road with a (5) .... on one side and a bus station opposite it. Beyond the (6) ...., in the distance, there is a (7) .... On the side of the square opposite the cathedral there's a (8) ...., and next to it there is a (9) .... There's another road going from the north-west corner of the square with a (10) .... on one side and a (11) .... next to it. On the other side of the road there's a (12) .... and beside the theatre there's a (13) .... This road goes past a (14) .... , which has got a (15) .... inside, and on the other side of the park, behind the cathedral, there's a (16) ....

2 All of the missing words in Exercise 2.1 were in the box in Exercise 1. Did you find them all? If not, look again for those you missed.

3 Now draw a plan of the city, including all the places mentioned.

3

1 Listen to four people talking about living in cities. Which speaker or speakers:

A likes city life?

B doesn't like city life?

C both likes and dislikes city life?

Speaker 1 ....   2 ....   3 ....   4 ....

2 Listen again and tick (✓) the words each speaker uses to describe life in cities.

> busy   dangerous   dirty   exciting   expensive
> fun   lively   noisy   stressful

3 Write two or three sentences about a town or city you know, using some of the words above.

Speaking

▶ **Part 2**

A friend is coming to spend the day with you. He wants to see as much as he can during his visit. Talk together about the things that you can do with your friend and then decide how to spend the day.

Hot tip!

In the exam, the examiner will read the instructions for the task to you twice. Listen carefully to the instructions both times so that you can complete the whole task.

Remember! *In this task you can choose more than one thing to do with your friend. Discuss each idea before deciding which ones to do.*

Reading

▶ **Part 4**

1

1 Add to the list below three more things that can cause litter.

fast food containers

....

....

....

2 Are there any places in your town where litter is a particular problem?

2

- Read the text and questions below.
- For each question, mark the letter next to the correct answer – **A**, **B**, **C** or **D**.

Looking after litter

When people just drop their unwanted paper and cans on the ground instead of putting them in rubbish bins, the streets end up full of litter. We are all responsible for this problem, as the litter is untidy and unpleasant for everyone. It can even become a danger when it's left in the streets for a long time. Dropping litter is actually a crime in some countries, and in Singapore you can be sent to prison for it. At Eatwell restaurants we think that the best thing to do about this problem is to teach people not to drop litter in the first place. Each Eatwell restaurant plays a part in educating the people who buy their food from us. Our restaurants help schools to do local 'clean-ups' of the area, and we also produce information sheets for our customers to read. As well as this, we provide more public litter bins throughout the country than most other companies, and we pick up litter around our own restaurants regularly. This is part of the promise we make to any town or area in which we operate.

1 What is the writer trying to do in this text?
  A explain why towns should provide more rubbish bins
  B complain about restaurants which cause litter
  C show how Eatwell restaurants are preventing litter
  D say why the food is so good in Eatwell restaurants

2 What can a reader find out from this text?
  A a punishment for dropping litter
  B how to collect rubbish
  C why rubbish is dangerous
  D countries where there is most litter

3 What does the writer think?
  A Restaurants are the main cause of litter.
  B Litter is an important problem for everyone.
  C People who drop litter should always be punished.
  D Teachers should tell their students to pick up litter.

4 How do Eatwell restaurants try to help the towns where they operate?
  A by giving teaching materials to local schools
  B by collecting litter from all over the town
  C by helping schools to buy food
  D by providing places for rubbish to be left

5 Which advertising sign shows the main idea of the text?

A
> We promise to provide good food and clean restaurants

B
> **We care for your town by helping to keep it clean**

C
> Education is the answer to all the world's problems

D
> Dropping litter is a crime – don't do it!

Reading

▶ Part 5

1 Read through the text below quickly. Don't fill in any spaces yet. What does the text describe?

a) the dangers of fire in cities

b) a fire in London in the past

c) the history of fire-fighting in London

d) ways of fighting fires in cities

2

• Read the text and choose the correct word for each space.

• For each question, mark the letter next to the correct word – **A**, **B**, **C** or **D**.

Remember! *Try to think what the word might be before you look at the four choices.*

A terrible fire

The original London Bridge (0) ....*was*........... built in about 1170. As (1) .... as providing a way across the River Thames, (2) .... was home to hundreds of families (3) .... lived in wooden houses on the bridge. There were also shops there, and even a church.

   One windy day in July 1212, fires started at both (4) .... of the bridge. The fires grew quickly and soon they had destroyed all the houses on the (5) ...., crowded street. About 3,000 people were killed on the bridge, or drowned in the river (6) .... People tried to (7) .... out the fires but they only had (8) .... to carry the water in, and in the end most of London was (9) .... down.

   Today, firefighters can (10) .... most fires. But in the past, many cities, including Moscow and Rome, have been partly destroyed by fire at least once.

0	A was	B is	C had	D has
1	A good	B far	C well	D long
2	A there	B that	C some	D it
3	A which	B where	C what	D who
4	A borders	B edges	C ends	D frontiers
5	A tight	B thin	C narrow	D slim
6	A under	B below	C through	D lower
7	A make	B have	C throw	D put
8	A bags	B purses	C boxes	D buckets
9	A burned	B fired	C smoked	D lighted
10	A change	B control	C command	D order

3 The fire on London Bridge was an important event in the history of the city. Do you know of any similar events in your own town or country? Discuss them with a partner.

4 The following events were all very important in world history. Do you know anything about them? Discuss each one with a partner and see how much you each know. Talk about

• what happened

• when it happened

• why it was important.

1 Columbus' voyage to America

2 Man landing on the Moon

3 The eruption of Vesuvius

Grammar

The past perfect

> We make the past perfect tense with *had* + past participle. We use it when we want to make it clear that something happened **before** a particular time in the past.

1   Find three examples of the past perfect in the text below and underline them.

By the time Jason was fifteen years old he had lived in four different countries and attended ten different schools. But he hadn't learned much in any of them. Had he enjoyed all this travelling around? He wasn't sure. He knew, however, that he didn't want to go abroad again and even now, at the age of 35, he refuses to leave England even for a short holiday.

2   Complete the sentences below. Write true information.

1 By the time I was seven, I had …
2 By the time I was twelve, I had …
3 By the time I was …, I had …

3   Number the events in each sentence in order. Put 1 for the event that happened first and 2 for the event that happened second. Then underline the time expression in each sentence.

Example:

[1] Underline When I had finished my meal, [2] I made a cup of coffee.

1 ☐ I did not do anything ☐ until I had received his letter.

2 ☐ I had just finished my homework ☐ when the phone rang.

3 ☐ As soon as I had had breakfast, ☐ I left the house.

4 ☐ Before I had even opened the door, ☐ I knew who was there.

5 ☐ I understood everything ☐ after I had read his letter.

6 ☐ After I had had my lunch, ☐ I had a short sleep.

4

Celia **had never been** to Paris before. This was **the first time she had been** to Paris.
first time + past perfect

*Bret **has never been** to Paris before. This is **the first time he has been** to Paris.*
first time + present perfect

Complete the sentences below using the correct form of the verb in brackets.

1 It was the first time in her life that Celia
.... (see) the Eiffel Tower.

2 Bret has seen the Eiffel Tower in films many times,
but it's the first time he .... (see) the real
thing.

5   Writing, Part 1

For each question, complete the second sentence
so that it means the same as the first. Use no more
than three words.

1 He finished his work before I arrived.
When I arrived, he .... his work.

2 I ate all the biscuits before teatime.
By teatime, I .... all the biscuits.

3 She knew how to drive a car when she was nine.
By the time she was nine, she had already ....
how to drive a car.

4 This is the first time she's been in trouble.
She's .... been in trouble before.

5 I had never stayed in such an expensive hotel before.
This was the first time I .... in such
an expensive hotel.

Reading

▶ **Part 1**

- Look at the text in each question.
- What does it say?
- Mark the letter next to the correct explanation
  – **A**, **B** or **C**.

> Please put your litter in
> the bins provided or take
> it home with you

1 A Don't leave your litter lying about.
  B You must take your litter home.
  D Don't take the bins home with you.

> **Stand on the
> right of the
> escalator to
> allow others
> to pass**

2 A You must pass other people standing on the
escalator.
  B You shouldn't stand on the left as other people
cannot pass you.
  C You mustn't pass other people on the right of the
escalator.

> *Dave*
> *Sue phoned – she's missed*
> *the bus and will be late. She'll be*
> *at the cinema at 6, not 5.30.*
> *Meet her there, not at home.*

3 A Sue will be too late to meet Dave.
  B Sue will go direct to the cinema at 6.
  C Dave must go home, not to the cinema.

Listening

▶ Part 1

- There are seven questions in this Part.
- For each question there are three pictures and a short recording.
- You will hear each recording twice.
- For each question, look at the pictures and listen to the recording.
- Choose the correct picture and put a tick (✓) in the box below it.

1   What is Susan going to wear?

   A ☐      B ☐      C ☐

2   Where does George live?

   A ☐      B ☐      C ☐

3   What are Kevin and Sally going to do tonight?

   A ☐      B ☐      C ☐

4   What is Sarah going to buy?

   A ☐      B ☐   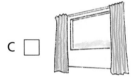   C ☐

5   Which picture are they looking at?

   A ☐   B ☐      C ☐

6   What present has Christine bought for the baby?

   A ☐      B ☐      C ☐

7   What is the man going to buy?

   A ☐      B ☐      C ☐

Writing

▶ Part 3: letter

1 Talk to a partner. Which of these things are there in or near the place where you live? What do they look like? What can you do there?

big buildings

old houses

good shops

new buildings

places to relax and enjoy yourself

historical monuments

Example:

> There's a big building in the middle of town. It's very high and very modern, and it's all glass. I quite like it, but my father hates it.

> There's a new sports centre outside town with a wonderful heated swimming pool and a big gym.

> The centre is quite old and there are lots of small streets with interesting little shops selling all sorts of things, and some very good cafés and restaurants where you can have a good meal quite cheaply.

2 Look at this writing task.

TASK

- This is part of a letter you receive from your English friend, Lorna.

  I really like the town where I live. How about you? Tell me about the town or city where you live.

- Now write a letter to Lorna telling her about the place where you live.

- Write about 100 words.

In your letter, you can describe the village, town or city where you live, say what you can do there and say whether you enjoy living there or not. Before you begin, look at Exercise 1 for ideas to write about.

Language spot

Useful phrases for letters:

Thanks for your letter. It was great to hear from you.
or *I was really pleased to get your letter.*

You asked me to tell you about ... so I'll do my best.

As well as that ...   What I like most is ...

Well, that's all I have time to write now ...

Write soon./Hope to hear from you soon./Keep in touch.

UNIT 12 Horror story

Vocabulary

1 Complete the crossword.

Clues across

1 The most dangerous hour of the night?
6 Her face was as white as a ....
8 They called the police to tell them they had found a dead ....
10 I heard a terrible .... which made my blood run cold.
12 You'd better not .... into the churchyard at night.
14 The joke was so .... that I couldn't stop laughing.
16 At the party, he did some .... tricks to amuse the children.
17 I'm going .... see a horror film. Do you want to come?

Clues down

2 Not nice.
3 If you saw one of these, you'd be frightened!
4 They said the horror film was based on a .... story.
5 The body of the murdered man was lying in a pool of ....
7 You must .... to find the answer to the mystery.
9 Some people .... at the sight of blood.
10 The book was .... exciting that I couldn't put it down.
11 'I'm doing a project about Houdini.' 'Who's he? I've never heard of ....'
13 *The Black Cat* is a horror story written .... Edgar Allen Poe.
15 'Do you believe in ghosts?' '.......... .'

2 Some adjectives end in either -ed or -ing. Many of these adjectives describe feelings.

When we say how a person is feeling, we use the -ed ending.

I was frightened (by the ghost).

When we are talking about the thing or situation that **causes** the feeling, we use the -ing ending.

The ghost was very frightening.

Add the correct ending to the adjective in each sentence.

1 Don't take your little sister to that film – it's too frighten.......... .

2 I was astonish.......... to hear that my brother had decided to go to America.

3 It's quite an amus.......... story, but I don't think it can be true.

4 The way they do the special effects in horror films is quite interest.......... .

5 I really enjoyed the film, but my boyfriend said he was bor.......... .

6 The special effects in that film are really amaz.......... .

7 This pizza tastes disgust........... . I don't know what they've done to it.

8 I invited my girlfriend to the cinema and then I found I'd left my money at home. I was really embarrass........... .

3 📼 Listen to six people talking about the book they are reading at present. What type of book is each one reading? Choose words from the box.

adventure story   detective story
horror story   love story
science fiction   thriller

1 ....

2 ....

3 ....

4 ....

5 ....

6 ....

Listening

▶ **Part 3**

1 📼

- Look at the notes about a seaside town.
- Some information is missing.
- You will hear part of a radio programme about the town.
- For each question, fill in the missing information in the numbered space.

Whitby...................

Town and (1) .... have existed here for almost 1,500 years

Now well known for connection with story of Dracula

The Dracula Experience

Unsuitable for (2) ....!

Contains electronic models of scenes from story including

– Dracula changing into a (3) ....

– Lucy (Dracula's (4) ....) who becomes a vampire

On Sea Front, facing harbour

Cost (5) .... (adults), £1.00 (children)

Other things to do

Climb 199 steps to St Mary's Church and churchyard

Visit Magpie Café for best (6) .... in England

2 **Writing: postcard**

Imagine you have just spent the day in Whitby. Write a postcard to a friend. In your postcard you should:

- describe something you saw in the town
- say what you thought of it
- explain what you will do next.

Write 35–45 words.

Reading

▶ **Part 4**

1

- Read the text and questions below.
- For each question, mark the letter next to the correct answer – **A**, **B**, **C** or **D**.

The Shining

Many people know the story of *The Shining* from the film starring Jack Nicholson, but few of them have read the book of the same name by Stephen King, the well-known writer of horror stories. He imagined the whole novel in his head while sitting up all night in the dark in the very same hotel where the story takes place, and then wrote it down, almost without stopping, over the next few days.

The story is seen through the eyes of a five-year-old boy called Danny who is a 'shiner' – he has special powers which he does not understand yet. His father, Jack, is taking care of an empty hotel far out in the country, which is closed for the winter. The hotel is completely cut off by a snowstorm, and Jack starts to behave more and more strangely ... and who are the strange guests in the supposedly empty room on the second floor? The heart of the book is not the hotel, however, but the way Jack and Danny feel about each other, and Jack's feelings about his own father.

The Shining is one of those rare novels that can burn itself into your brain. I think it is possible that it is one of the best horror novels ever written.

1 What is the writer trying to do in this text?
   A describe Jack Nicholson's performance in *The Shining*
   B explain why Stephen King is such a good writer
   C give his opinion of the book *The Shining*
   D say why Stephen King's book is better than the film

2 What can the reader learn about the way the story was written?
   A The idea came to the writer in a dream.
   B The story was all written in one night.
   C The writer was describing real people.
   D The writer got the idea from a real place.

3 What does the writer think about Stephen King's book?
   A It is difficult to forget this story.
   B It is very different from the film.
   C It is the best horror story he has ever read.
   D The book can be dangerous for nervous people.

4 What is the main idea of the book?
   A how people behave when they are alone
   B how the weather changes the way people behave
   C how family members can feel about each other
   D how a child can have special powers

5 Which person is talking about Stephen King's book?

A *It's really frightening – in the book, the whole story takes place in a hotel in just one night.*

B *It's clever the way the writer shows you how a young child sees the world.*

C *The writer lets you know what the father is thinking – the whole story is from his point of view.*

D *It's interesting to learn about all the different guests who come to stay in the hotel.*

2   What's the most frightening book/film you know? Compare your ideas with a partner.

Grammar

It is and *there is*

> We use *it* to refer to:
>
> * something definite in the previous sentence
>   Go to **the Royal Hotel. It** is the best hotel in town.
> * something that comes later in that sentence.
>   **It is** a dictionary.
>   **It is** difficult **to find the answer**.
>
> We also use *it* to talk about the time, date and weather.
> It's six o'clock.
> It's Monday January 25.
> It's snowing today.
>
> We use *There is/There are* to introduce new information.
> There is a hotel in the town.
> There are some eggs in the fridge.
> There's something burning.

1   Fill in the gaps using *There* or *It*.

1 .... is someone at the door.

2 .... is quite warm today.

3 .... is boring to go for a walk on your own.

4 .... are some good programmes on television tonight.

5 .... is nothing to do here.

6 You should go to that film. ....'s really exciting.

2   Fill in the gaps to make pairs of sentences with the same meaning.

1
a) It is difficult to put this book down.
b) This book .... to put down.

2
a) The end is easy to guess.
b) .... easy .... guess the end.

3
a) .... to find the answer.
b) The answer is hard to find.

4
a) Finding a hotel was easy.
b) It .... easy to .... a hotel.

5
a) There is a black dog sleeping in the garden.
b) A black dog .... in the garden.

6
a) .... lots of people .... to get in.
b) Lots of people are waiting to get in.

3   Writing, Part 1

Here are some sentences about entertainment. For each question, complete the second sentence so that it means the same as the first. Use no more than three words.

1 They say the film has some frightening scenes.
They say .... some frightening scenes in the film.

2 I have not been to a horror film before.
It is .... I've ever been to a horror film.

3 She said, 'I'm not very interested in card tricks.'
'I don't think card tricks are ....,' she said.

4 She asked if I wanted to go to the theatre with her.
She said, ' .... to go to the theatre with me?'

5 The film was shorter than I had expected.
The film was not .... I had expected.

Reading

▶ **Part 5**

1   Read through the text quickly. Don't fill in any spaces yet. Why was Houdini famous?

A   He travelled all over the world.

B   He could escape from difficult places.

C   He won a lot of money playing cards.

2

- Read the text and choose the correct word for each space.

- For each question, mark the letter next to the correct word – **A**, **B**, **C** or **D**.

Houdini

Harry Houdini was born in 1874 in Budapest, (0) .....*but*..... when he was four his family moved to America. They were very poor, and so he left school (1) .... the age of twelve and got a job selling newspapers. When he was a teenager he began (2) .... card tricks, and soon he was giving performances of magic in (3) .... In 1894 he met his wife, a dancer, and they got married after only two weeks.

Soon (4) .... Houdini started the escape acts which made him famous. He would ask people to lock him up in different (5) ...., and he always (6) .... to escape. He escaped from strong chains, locked boxes (7) .... of water, and even a big paper bag (without tearing the paper). (8) .... of his last performances (9) .... to escape after being buried (10) .... No one ever found out how he did it.

0	A but	B so	C because	D or
1	A on	B at	C with	D to
2	A saying	B having	C making	D doing
3	A theatre	B public	C crowd	D television
4	A before	B afterwards	C later	D next
5	A methods	B reasons	C forms	D ways
6	A succeeded	B could	C managed	D meant
7	A full	B packed	C crowded	D complete
8	A Some	B All	C Each	D One
9	A tried	B had	C was	D happened
10	A alive	B live	C living	D awake

Reading

▶ **Part 1**

- Look at the text in each question.

- What does it say?

- Mark the letter next to the correct explanation – **A**, **B** or **C**.

> Register your email address with us to receive up-to-date booking information for new shows.

1   A   You can book theatre tickets by email.

　　B   You can find out if tickets are available for new shows.

　　C   You can get a book of information about new shows.

> **This film contains scenes that may be unsuitable for children under 12.**

2   A   Children under 12 cannot see this film.

　　B   Children over 12 will not find this film suitable.

　　D   The film is not recommended for children under 12.

Writing

▶ Part 3: story

Write a story beginning with this sentence:

It was nearly midnight and the moon was almost hidden by dark clouds.

Write about 100 words. Think about:

The beginning

- the person or people
- the place
- the feelings

The middle

- a problem or a mystery

The ending

Remember this is the most important part of your story!

It will probably make your story more interesting if you include the following:

- some description at the beginning to set the scene
- some speech.

To help you with some ideas for the description, choose some words and phrases from the box to describe the picture above.

cold	windy	frightening	too quiet
strange noises		a bit spooky	a bit unreal

To help you with some ideas for the speech, choose the best thing to say if:

1 you suddenly hear a strange noise.

   a Who's there?

2 you think you see a strange person.

   b What's that?

3 you are frightened.

   c Where are you?

4 you can't find your friend.

   d Somebody help me!

> ### Hot tip!
>
> It is often a good idea to end your story with a very short sentence. This has a strong effect on the reader.

Speaking

▶ Part 2

Look at the task below.

> You are going out to the cinema with your friends and their younger brothers and sisters. You are trying to decide what type of film to see that you will all enjoy. Talk together about the different types of films you could go to and then decide which one to see.

Think about the advantages and disadvantages of the different types of films for all the family (including children). Then discuss the task with a partner. Remember to talk about all the different types of film before you decide which one is the best.

▶ **Part 3**

The pictures below show different ways in which people find excitement in their lives.
Work with a partner. Choose one of the pictures. Describe:

- what you can see
- how the people might be feeling and why.

Remember! *Talk for about a minute.*

Now ask your partner to describe the other picture in the same way.

▶ **Part 4**

Talk with your partner about the things that you find interesting or exciting, and the things you find boring.

Hot tip!

Remember to respond to what your partner says, and to ask them questions. Do not just give your own opinion – this is a conversation!

Practice exam

PAPER 1 – READING AND WRITING

Reading

PART 1

Questions 1–5

Look at the text in each question.

What does it say?

Mark the correct letter, – **A**, **B** or **C**.

In the actual exam you will mark your answers **on the separate answer sheet**.

Example:

0

PLEASE COMPLETE THE FORM IN CAPITAL
LETTERS USING **BLACK** INK

A Use a pen with black ink and write in capital letters.

B Write your name on the form in capital letters.

C You must sign this form in black ink.

Answer:

1

Please be quiet in
this corridor – exam
in progress in
the library

A Don't make a noise when you enter the library.

B Wait quietly in the corridor until you are told to begin the exam.

C Don't disturb students taking the exam in the library.

2

Please remember
to lock the
door behind you
when you leave
the building

A Don't leave the building without locking the door.

B Don't lock the door when you are in the building.

C Don't leave the building by the back door.

3

Please don't turn this computer off – I'm still working on it. Please use the one in the corner. Back in five minutes!

A The computer should be turned off in five minutes.

B There is another computer available for use.

C Wait five minutes before using the computer.

4

Receive regular information about the Ice Centre by filling in the form below.

A If you fill in the form, you can use the Ice Centre.

B We will send you a form with information about the Ice Centre.

C Fill in the form to get up-to-date information about the Ice Centre.

5

ICE ON ROADS
– DANGEROUS
DRIVING
CONDITIONS
UNTIL MORNING

A There will be ice on the roads in the morning.

B It will be impossible to drive on some roads tonight.

C Be careful of the ice on the roads during the night.

PART 2

Questions 6–10

The people below all want to rent a video to watch.

On the opposite page there are descriptions of eight videos.

Decide which video would be most suitable for each person or family.

For questions **6–10**, mark the correct letter (**A–H**).

In the actual exam you will mark your answers **on the separate answer sheet**.

6  Janey is a drama student. She likes reading true stories, especially about the theatre. She prefers stories and films that have a happy ending.

7  Sarah and Chris want a video they can enjoy watching with their two sons aged ten and twelve. The boys like adventure and lots of action.

8  Trudi, 13, enjoys reading teenage magazines and school stories. She likes animals, especially horses, but hates childish films.

9  John is an engineer. He likes true-life stories and is interested in anything to do with machines, but he won't watch anything with singing or dancing in.

10  Nick is organising a children's party for his son's fourth birthday. He's planned lots of games, and there will be food and drink. He wants a video that's not too long or noisy for the children to watch after they've had their food.

A

From the horse's mouth 75 mins

When Dobbin the horse learns to speak, there's trouble on the farm. Young children have been enjoying this cartoon film for the last 40 years, and it has one of the most exciting and fast-moving endings around.

B

Moon landing 136 mins

Although most people who remember the real moon landing will know what is going to happen in this film, the events are still exciting. Will Sykes plays the captain trying to get his men back to Earth alive when technical problems put all their lives in danger. A real-life story which is sometimes difficult to follow, but worth the effort.

C

Elvis! 136 mins

Based on the true story of Elvis Presley, the film shows his amazing success as a young man, with original recordings of some of his greatest songs, but it is at its best in the second half where we follow his troubled personal life and the health problems of his later years.

D

Danger ahead 112 mins

Starting in New York in the present day, this fast-moving science fiction film moves quickly into the future. The amazing scenes of spaceships flying over New York have to be seen (and heard) to be believed! Not for those who want a story they can believe in, but first-class entertainment for both young and old.

E

Sing to the top 141 mins

This film of the amazing real life story of Sylvia Stebbs won the prize for best musical of the year. Set in Hollywood in the 1930s, it tells the story of how Sylvia rises to become one of the most famous singers and actresses of her day.

F

Magic class 121 mins

Amy-Beth needs some magic in her life – but she's not too successful when she goes to evening classes in Magic Studies. When she tries to use her special knowledge to make the boy next door fall in love with her, the results are out of this world!

G

Captain Cheese saves the day 30 mins

This story follows the adventures of Captain Cheese, a mouse with special powers who meets a lion with a big problem – he's lost his voice. A peaceful, gentle story, very different from most other children's cartoons.

H

The black shoes 135 mins

When Igor finds a pair of black ballet shoes, he gives them to Natasha, his dancing partner, and she finds they fit her perfectly. Wearing the shoes, she dances as she has never done before, until the horrifying final performance. Not suitable for children under 15.

PART 3

Questions 11–20

Look at the sentences below about a zoo.
Read the text on the opposite page to decide if each sentence is correct or incorrect.
If it is correct, mark **A**.
If it is not correct, mark **B**.

In the actual exam you will mark your answers **on the separate answer sheet**.

11   The zoo is just outside the town of Seaport.

12   Visitors to the zoo can go swimming in a pool with dolphins.

13   You can get off the 'Animal Train' in different parts of the zoo.

14   Children must be with an adult when they go to the children's zoo.

15   Posters at the main entrance give details of animal feeding times.

16   Zoo workers finish their work at 6.00 p.m.

17   The animals are fed at eight o'clock in the morning.

18   Older children can help the keepers to look after the elephants.

19   In summer there are four places where you can buy presents and souvenirs.

20   You can reach the zoo by bus or by car.

Welcome to Seaport Zoo

Seaport Zoo is only two miles from the centre of Seaport, one of Britain's most popular holiday towns. Set in beautiful countryside, it is home to over 400 animals from all over the world, including lions, tigers and elephants. It also has many special attractions, including Monkey Mountain and our new 'Dolphin-mobile', a special boat which allows you to get close to the dolphins in their sea-water pool.

Visitors of all ages will enjoy a ride on the 'Animal Train' which travels from the main entrance to the far side of the zoo. It passes through beautiful woodland and offers views of some of our animals. There are stops near all the main attractions, including our children's zoo, which gives our young visitors the chance to touch and maybe even feed some of our smaller animals. Please note that children are not allowed in this area unless they are with an adult.

The work in the zoo is non-stop and our staff make sure that the animals get all the care and attention they need. The first job of the day is to clean the animals' homes – this starts at eight o'clock and has to be done every day, to make sure that the animals are kept happy and healthy. We feed the animals at the zoo six bags of carrots, six boxes of bananas, eight boxes of apples and ten bags of potatoes every week. The zoo gates close at 6 p.m. but the work still goes on as there are plenty more things to do before bedtime. The last job of the day is to feed the elephants their supper, and then it's goodnight and sleep tight.

If you want to know more about your favourite animal, then come along to one of the short talks given by our staff. The talks change every day, so check the posters at the main entrance to make sure you don't miss anything. Or for something really different, why not try an 'Elephant Experience'? Helped by our fully-trained keepers, you can actually help wash and feed these wonderful animals. Note: You must be at least 16 years of age for an 'Elephant Experience'.

The zoo has a large restaurant, and drinks and snacks can also be bought from machines next to the picnic area. In addition, a gift shop is open throughout the year at the main entrance. Two smaller gift shops are also opened during the summer.

The zoo is open every day from 10 a.m. to 6 p.m. There is a large car park, and in addition regular buses run between Seaport Station and the zoo.

PART 4

Questions 21–25

Read the text and questions below.

For each question, mark the correct letter, **A**, **B**, **C** or **D**.

In the actual exam you will mark your answers on the separate answer sheet.

POP STAR

You need the right songs and a good voice to be a pop star, but you also need to be a great performer – and it's an advantage if you can dance well, especially if you want to be part of a group. To be successful, you have to be a special kind of person as well as a good singer. People will only notice you if you have a different 'look', but at the same time you need to keep your own identity. All those long hours travelling between interviews and photo shoots will make you very tired, but you must always be warm and friendly, because if people don't like you, you won't get far. They won't put pictures of you in their magazines, they won't ask you to come on their television shows and they won't play your CDs. You must be super-confident because you'll be meeting lots of new people regularly – from interviews with journalists to chatting on television shows. It's your job to sell yourself – you've got to have something to say, and your attitude is really important! You have to want to be famous, and be prepared to work extremely hard at it. It's not going to be easy!

---

21   What is the writer trying to do in this text?

    A   give information about people who are pop stars

    B   explain why being a pop star is not a safe job

    C   explain why he or she wants to be a pop star

    D   give advice on how to become a pop star

22   What can a reader learn from this text?

    A   Pop stars must always look up to date.

    B   Pop stars have to be good dancers as well as good singers.

    C   Pop stars need to get on well with people.

    D   Pop stars have more free time than other people.

23 What does the writer say about being a pop star?

   A It's a wonderful job.

   B It's difficult.

   C It can make you very rich.

   D It can be very lonely.

24 The writer talks about travelling to show that

   A being a pop star is tiring.

   B a pop star's life is expensive.

   C pop stars are often on their own.

   D pop stars see a lot of the world.

25 Which person is the most likely to become a successful pop star?

A

I love dancing, and going out with my friends. I think being a pop star would be great – nothing to do but sing and wear lovely clothes!

B

I like dancing and I love singing – but my studies are important too. But that's no problem – I could study in the day, and sing at concerts in the evening.

C

I love going places and meeting people and I can't wait to be famous – it's all I want to do!

D

I'm a bit nervous when I meet people I don't know – but everyone says I have a really good voice.

PART 5

Questions 26–35

Read the text below and choose the correct word for each space.
For each question, mark the correct letter, **A**, **B**, **C** or **D**.

In the actual exam you will mark your answers on the separate answer sheet.

Example:

0   A out   B at   C on   D in

Answer: 0 [A ▬] [B ▭] [C ▭] [D ▭]

AN AMAZING PILL

Doctors have a new way to find (**0**) .... what is happening in your stomach.
All you (**26**) .... to do is take a small pill. The pill, which is about the same
(**27**) .... as a thumb nail, contains a light and a video camera. When it gets to the
stomach, the camera starts to (**28**) .... pictures which are recorded by equipment on a
special belt (**29**) .... around the patient's stomach. The pill can (**30**) ....
to work for up to seven hours and can be used to see (**31**) .... the patient has any
stomach problems (**32**) .... as bleeding. The amazing tablet was (**33**) ....
by the American space agency NASA, and can certainly go where no medical equipment has gone
before! Doctors say that it is a (**34**) .... cheaper and safer way of discovering the
(**35**) .... of stomach pain than having an operation.

---

26   A must   B should   C have   D can

27   A taste   B size   C use   D type

28   A take   B make   C show   D paint

29   A carried   B worn   C shown   D dressed

30   A continue   B keep   C press   D move

31   A as   B unless   C whether   D because

32   A like   B same   C such   D so

33   A done   B found   C built   D invented

34   A very   B most   C much   D more

35   A causes   B reasons   C directions   D places

Writing

PART 1

Questions 1–5

Here are some sentences about a holiday by the sea.

For each question, complete the second sentence so that it means the same as the first.

Use no more than three words.

Write only the missing words.

In the actual exam you will write your answers **on the separate answer sheet**.

Example:

0   My house is a long way from the nearest beach.

There isn't a beach .... my house.

Answer: | **0** | *near* |

1   I have never visited this beach before.

It is .... that I have ever visited this beach.

2   My friend said that she thought it was a good place.

My friend said, '... it is a good place.'

3   However, the weather's colder than I expected.

However, the weather's not .... I expected.

4   I can't go swimming because the waves are so big.

The waves are too big for .... swimming.

5   I am not having a very good time.

I am not .... myself very much.

PART 2

Question 6

An English friend of yours called Stephanie has sent you a birthday present.

Write an email to Stephanie. In your email, you should:

- thank her for her present

- say why you like it

- tell her what you did on your birthday.

Write **35–45 words**.

In the actual exam you will write your answers **on the separate answer sheet**.

PART 3

Write an answer to **one** of the questions (**7** or **8**) in this part.

Write your answer in about **100 words**.

In the actual exam you will write your answer **on the separate answer sheet** and put the question number in the box at the top of your answer sheet.

Question 7

- This is part of a letter you receive from your English penfriend.

I've just joined a new sports club. It's very good.

What sort of sports do you like?

- Now write a letter to your penfriend telling him or her about the sports you like.

- Write your **letter** on your answer sheet.

Question 8

- Your English teacher has asked you to write a story.

- Your story must have the following title:

  A happy day

- Write your **story** on your answer sheet.

PAPER 2 – LISTENING

PART 1

Questions 1–7

There are seven questions in this part.

For each question there are three pictures and a short recording.

Choose the correct picture and put a tick (✓) in the box below it.

Example: What time does the performance begin?

A ☐   B ☐   C ☑

1   What is the man's job now?

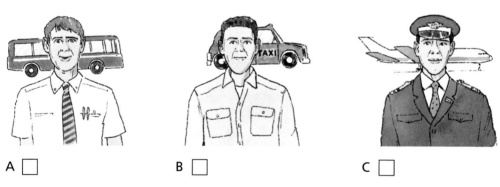

A ☐   B ☐   C ☐

2   What will the woman post?

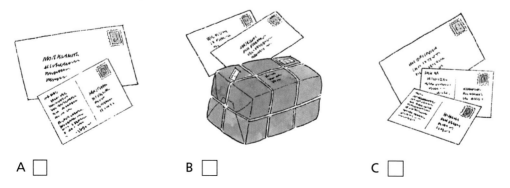

A ☐   B ☐   C ☐

3 What kind of holiday is the man going to have?

A ☐   B ☐   C ☐

4 Why does the man need to see the doctor?

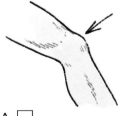  

A ☐   B ☐   C ☐

5 What does the boy decide to buy?

A ☐   B ☐   C ☐

6 Which is the girl's room?

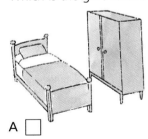  

A ☐   B ☐   C ☐

7 What is the man having a problem with at present?

  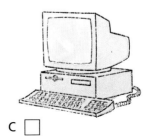

A ☐   B ☐   C ☐

PART 2

Questions 8–13

You will hear a woman talking on local radio about a local festival.
For each question, put a tick (✓) in the correct box.

8 The Chelford festival was first held

A seven years ago. ☐
B eight years ago. ☐
C ten years ago. ☐

9 The festival will be opened by

A a pop singer. ☐
B a local actress. ☐
C a radio announcer. ☐

10 What is the first prize for the quiz?

A a year's free cinema tickets ☐
B a camera and free film ☐
C a short holiday in London ☐

11 Chelford lemon curd is similar to

A jam. ☐
B cake. ☐
C cream cheese. ☐

12 The dessert for the meal on Saturday evening will be

A fruit and ice-cream. ☐
B fruit and cream. ☐
C ice-cream only. ☐

13 Joe Stanton's band will be playing on Saturday evening

A before the meal. ☐
B during the meal. ☐
C at the disco. ☐

PART 3

Questions 14–19

You will hear a tour leader talking about how to be safe when skiing.

For each question, fill in the missing information in the numbered space.

Ski Holidays Unlimited

Name of tour leader: (14) ....

Rules for safety while skiing:

Don't

- go skiing (15) ....

- go on ski runs that are (16) ....

Do

- wear warm clothes and use (17) ....

- leave mountain before (18) ....

Tour leader available in hotel reception every day from (19) .... a.m.

PART 4

Questions 20–25

Look at the six sentences for this part.

You will hear a conversation between a girl, Megan, and a boy, Jim, about something they have to do in class.

Decide if each sentence is correct or incorrect.

If it is correct, put a tick (✓) in the box under **A** for **YES**. If it is not correct, put a tick (✓) in the box under **B** for **NO**.

		A YES	B NO
20	Megan missed class today because she went to the dentist.	☐	☐
21	Megan was in class when the teacher first said they had to give a talk.	☐	☐
22	Megan feels pleased that she is giving the talk with Jim next week.	☐	☐
23	In the talk they just have to say what happens in a book.	☐	☐
24	Jim would prefer to talk about a thriller.	☐	☐
25	Jim agrees to read a novel at the weekend.	☐	☐

PAPER 3 – SPEAKING

PART 1 (2–3 minutes)

Where do you come from?

What's your name? How do you spell it?

What do you enjoy doing at the weekends?

Do you work or are you a student?

What kind of sport do you enjoy?

Why are you studying English ?

What do you enjoy about learning English?

PART 2 (2–3 minutes)

One of your friends has a birthday soon and you want to plan a surprise for him or her on the day. Talk together about the things that you could do and then decide what to do for the day.

PART 3 (1 minute each)

The photographs below show people enjoying the countryside. Show the photograph to your partner and talk about it.

PART 4 (3 minutes)

Your photographs showed people enjoying themselves outside. I'd like you to talk together about the things you like to do outside at different times of the day.

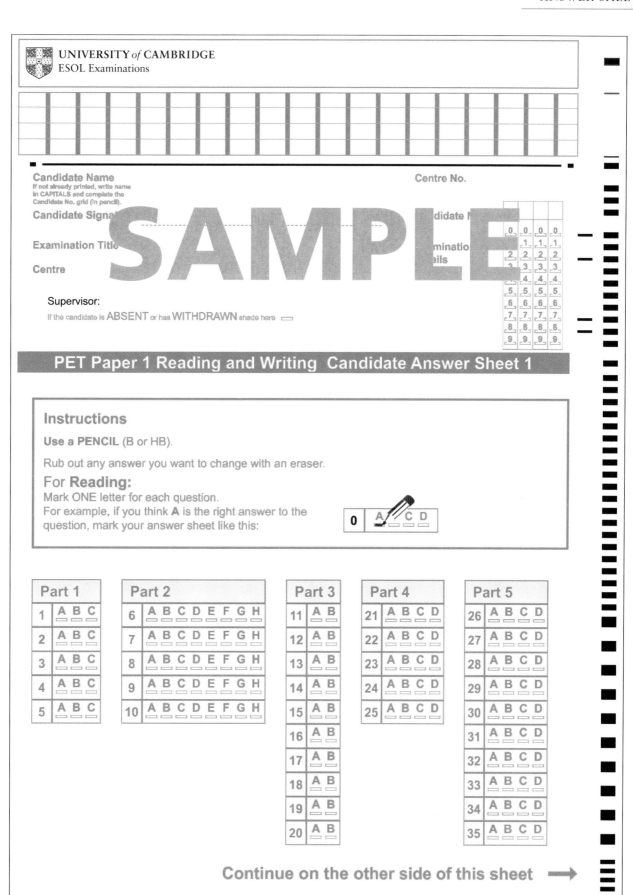

For **Writing (Parts 1 and 2):**

Write your answers clearly in the spaces provided.

SAMPLE

Part 1: Write your answers below.

		Do not write here
1		1 1 0
2		1 2 0
3		1 3 0
4		1 4 0
5		1 5 0

Part 2 (Question 6): Write your answer below.

Put your answer to Writing Part 3 on Answer Sheet 2 ➡

Do not write below (Examiner use only).

0	1	2	3	4	5

Part 3: Mark the number of the question you are answering here ➡ Q7 or Q8

Write your answer below.

SAMPLE

Do not write below this line

This section for use by SECOND Examiner only

Mark:

0	1.1	1.2	1.3	2.1	2.2	2.3	3.1	3.2	3.3	4.1	4.2	4.3	5.1	5.2	5.3

Examiner Number:

	0 1 2 3 4 5 6 7 8 9
	0 1 2 3 4 5 6 7 8 9
	0 1 2 3 4 5 6 7 8 9
	0 1 2 3 4 5 6 7 8 9

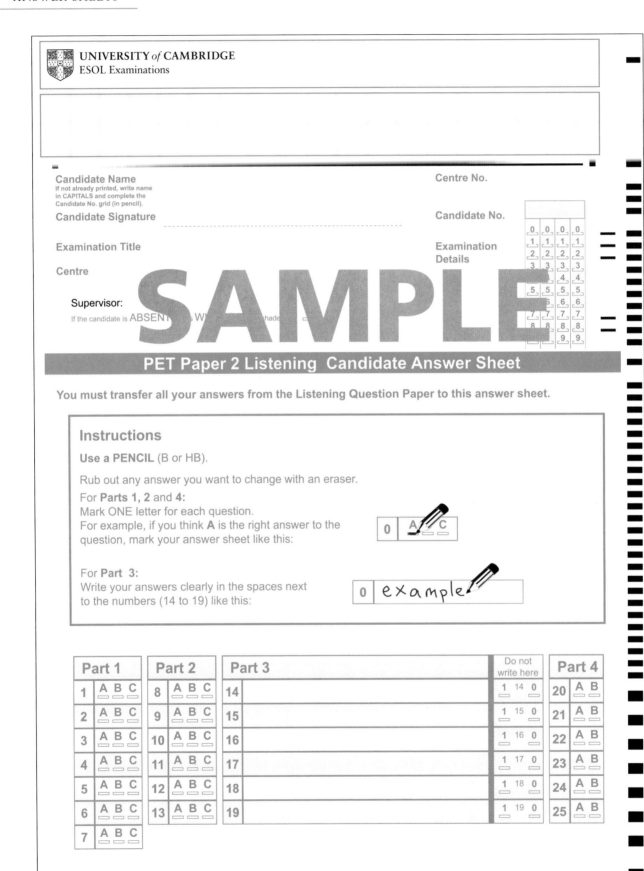

Teacher's notes

The PET exam

The PET exam tests the use of language in real-life situations. It tests the student's ability in the four components of Reading, Writing, Listening and Speaking. The exam is based on the Council of Europe Threshold Level, and is approximately two thirds of the way towards the First Certificate in English.

At this level a student should be able to cope in a range of everyday situations which require a largely predictable use of language. They should be able to deal with authentic materials, such as public notices, guides and magazine articles. As tourists, they should be able to get all the necessary information from information centres, understand a commentary and ask questions to get more information. They should not be expected to deal with technical language. At work they can describe their own job area, exchange factual information, receive instructions and deal with telephone messages. They can write personal letters within a standard format.

Aims of PET

The assessment aims of PET and its syllabus are designed to make sure that the test reflects the use of language in real life. It corresponds closely to an active and communicative approach to learning English, although it still places importance on clarity and accuracy. The successful candidate should be able to communicate satisfactorily in most everyday situations with both native and non-native speakers of English. This aim corresponds to the recommendations of the Council of Europe's Threshold Specification.

Assessment and marking

The four skills components are tested in three papers. Each component carries 25% of the final mark. The actual scores are weighted to achieve this balance. There is no minimum pass mark for individual papers. There are two passing grades, Pass with Merit (approximately 85% of the total mark) and Pass (approximately 70% of the total mark). There are also two failing grades, Narrow Fail (within 5% of Pass mark) and Fail.

Paper 1 Reading and Writing 1 hour 30 mins

The Reading component of Paper 1 has five separate parts. There are 35 questions which test a broad range of reading skills. Each question has one mark, and the student's score is then converted to a final mark which is 25% of the whole examination.

The Writing component has three parts. Part 1 has five related questions which have one mark each. In Part 2, candidates have to produce a short communicative message, which is marked out of 5. It is marked according to marking schemes that include task achievement. In Part 3, candidates can choose to write a letter or a story, which is marked out of 15. It is marked according to marking schemes that include range and accuracy of language, and text organisation. This gives a total mark of 25 for the Writing component of Paper 1, which represents 25% of the whole examination.

Paper 2 Listening 30 mins

The Listening paper has four parts with 25 questions. There is one mark for each question.

Paper 3 Speaking 10–12 mins

There are four parts with 30 marks, weighted to 25.

Assessment of Speaking

The Speaking test involves two examiners and two candidates. One examiner asks the questions (the interlocutor) and the other is the assessor. The assessor does not take part in the conversation. Students are assessed throughout on their language skills, not their knowledge of the world. They need to show:

- a range of grammar and vocabulary, used accurately and appropriately
- good discourse management (i.e. they should link ideas together and be able to produce a sequence of linked ideas)
- good pronunciation (although this does not have to be perfect, it should be comprehensible)
- interactive communication (they should take turns at speaking, ask their partner questions and respond to what their partner says).

The assessor gives a mark out of five for each of these four areas. The interlocutor gives a global impression mark out of ten, making a maximum of 30. The mark is then converted to a final total out of 25.

Note: In the PET exam the use of American pronunciation, spelling and vocabulary is acceptable.

Topics

- Clothes
- Daily life
- Education
- Entertainment and media
- Family and relations with other people
- Food and drink
- Free time
- Health, medicine and exercise
- Hobbies and leisure
- House and home
- Language
- Personal identification
- Places and buildings
- Services
- Shopping
- Sport
- The natural world
- Transport
- Travel and holidays
- Weather
- Work and jobs

Key functions, notions and communicative tasks in both speaking and writing

- Greeting people and responding to greetings
- Understanding and writing letters giving personal details
- Asking and answering questions about personal possessions
- Asking for and giving the spelling and meaning of words
- Talking about future plans or intentions
- Asking for and giving simple information about routines and habits
- Giving advice
- Expressing opinions and making choices
- Talking about ability and inability in the past or present
- Talking about possibility and impossibility
- Describing simple processes
- Describing people (personal appearance, qualities)
- Understanding and producing simple narratives

Lexis

The PET vocabulary list includes items which occur normally in the everyday vocabulary of native speakers. Students should know words that are appropriate for expressing personal information and opinions, such as hobbies, likes and dislikes.

Teaching procedures and advice

The *PET Gold Exam Maximiser* helps students in all the key areas of the exam in a clear, graded and systematic way. Here are some ideas for teaching the skills of reading and listening as well as presenting grammar and vocabulary.

General procedures for reading and listening

The exam tests a variety of reading and listening skills through multiple-choice questions, matching and gap-fill activities. The texts are all taken from real life. To help prepare students for these parts of the exam, it is a good idea to give them a lot of different texts to read, including simple articles, reviews, instructions, descriptions and stories. Using simplified readers can also give your students confidence, and they will enjoy reading them. Encourage students to listen to as much English as possible inside and outside the classroom, e.g. songs, DVDs, videos and TV programmes.

Lead-in activities

Before reading a text or listening to a recording, it is a good idea to prepare students for what they will read or hear. Students need to think about what they already know about the topic, and in some cases it may be necessary to revise or pre-teach specific vocabulary. (However, it is not a good idea to pre-teach all new vocabulary in the text as students need to develop their own strategies for dealing with new words.) In addition, exam students need preparation for the task itself. Many of the reading and listening activities in the *PET Gold Exam Maximiser* already have lead-in activities and more ideas are given below (page 132). In addition, here are some general ideas that can be used with any reading or listening activity.

- **Using the title or general topic**

1 Put the title or a key word on the board with the letters in jumbled order in each word. Students guess the words, e.g. (a country) AATSILRAU.
2 Put the title on the board with some letters missing, e.g. (a country) A _ _ T _ _ _ I A.
3 Put the title on the board with one word missing and see if the students can predict the missing word, e.g. .... in Australia.
4 Put the title on the board and brainstorm what sort of information the text might be about, e.g. Travelling in Australia.
5 Make up simple general-knowledge questions on the topic (see Unit 7 Reading Part 2 questions on New Zealand). These can be yes/no questions or true/false questions.
6 Relate the topic to the students' own situation. For example, if a text is about restaurants, begin by asking them about restaurants in their own town.

- **Using words from the text or tapescript**

1 Choose five or six key words from the text or tapescript and ask students to make up sentences using two or three of these words (see Teacher's Notes Unit 6 Reading Part 4).
2 Choose pairs of words from the text, write them in two columns jumbled, and see if students can match them. For example, from Unit 1 Reading Part 3:

oil	*friends*
science	*hair*
best	*painting*
red	*fiction*

Students then check the text for the correct answers before doing the task.
3 Choose key words from the text related to the main topic, and mix them up with some other words on different

topics. See if students can identify which words don't fit the main topic.

- **Using pictures**

Wherever possible, bring extra pictures into class related to the topic, e.g. pictures of holiday scenes or pictures of people. This helps to stimulate the students' interest and is also good practice for the Speaking paper.

You can also introduce a topic by drawing a simple picture on the board. For example, for Unit 1 Reading Part 2, you could begin by drawing a stick figure of a boy sitting at a computer. Ask the students to guess what you are drawing as you do so, e.g. *Is this a boy or a girl? How old is he/she? What's he doing?* (The activity is more fun if your drawing isn't very good!)

Doing the reading task

Students should read through the text silently, following the guidelines given for specific task types in the book. They should be encouraged not to use dictionaries while doing the tasks, although they may check new words and expressions afterwards. When they have finished a task, they can check their answers with a partner. Discussing the answers will help them to think about the strategies they have used and will encourage them to learn from one another. When checking answers, encourage students to say where they found their answers. The answer key gives extra help with correct and incorrect answers.

After reading

In the *PET Gold Exam Maximiser* there are often questions at the end of an activity which personalise the topic by, for example, asking the students to say whether they would like to visit this place or do something similar to the things the text describes. Don't leave out these short activities! They give valuable speaking practice and help the students to apply the language to their own experiences.

You can also ask more questions to get a personal reaction, e.g.

Which place would you most like to visit? Why?
Which thing sounds most exciting/dangerous/ enjoyable/frightening?
Would you like to meet this person? What questions would you ask him/her?
How does this place/situation compare with your country?

Finally, it is extremely useful to ask students to identify key phrases and record these to use later on. For example, Unit 1 Reading Part 3:
playing the drums, most of the time, have a great time, brilliant at science, not so keen on work.

General procedures for writing

It is difficult for students to move from writing individual sentences to producing simple letters or stories. The *PET Gold*

Exam Maximiser provides practice in typical real-life writing tasks, such as writing out phone messages and writing short letters to a friend. These give students a real reason for writing. It is also a good idea to ask them to keep a diary, which they can write in regularly and show to the teacher. This will take away the fear of writing beyond sentence level and get them into the habit of writing typical PET tasks.

Marking should be done carefully in order to give students confidence in their writing ability and to develop their ability to self-correct. Teachers should refer to the marking criteria on page 129 and should give marks for task achievement as well as for language. The *PET Handbook*, available from University of Cambridge ESOL Examinations, gives a more detailed breakdown of marking criteria together with sample marked answers. Mistakes which interfere with communication should always be corrected, but credit should also be given to students who try to use more complex language, even if this is not always accurate.

When giving feedback to the class on writing tasks, discuss different ways of saying the same thing and look at phrases or sentences with similar meanings. This will help the students with Writing Part 1 (the transformations) as well as with the other writing tasks.

General procedures for speaking

The students do the Speaking exam in pairs. It is therefore vital that they do plenty of pairwork activities in class. This will give them the opportunity to develop fluency and interactive skills. Do not worry if they make grammatical mistakes while doing these pairwork activities – it is more important that they develop confidence, and perfect grammar is not expected in the exam at this level.

Some students may be shy about expressing their own opinions and in these cases, it may help to give them a role to play – for example, a tourist guide.

Suggestions for additional activities

Unit 1

Reading p.8

Lead-in (books closed)
Discuss the idea of a personal website. This is a series of 'pages' that people can put on the internet giving information about themselves through words and pictures. Ask students what sort of information they might put on their own website, e.g. family, friends, interests, likes and dislikes. (**Note:** Contact details such as addresses and telephone numbers are **not** normally given on this type of website for security reasons.)

Follow-up activities
Students make a family tree of Joe and his family.
Students draw three empty squares on a piece of paper and

imagine that each square is a photograph or picture on their own website. They explain to a partner what is in each 'picture' and why they have chosen it.

Students look for similar websites on their computers at home and bring printouts into class.

Students make their own real (or paper) websites.

Grammar p.13

Oral activity

Ask the class to tell you some of the possessions they have or would like to have, e.g. mobile phone, portable TV, playstation, DVD player, guitar, set of drums, lap-top computer.

Write the words in a circle on the board. Students take turns to make sentences (orally), comparing two or three of the objects, e.g. *A mobile phone's cheaper than a lap-top computer. The drums are probably the noisiest.*

The same activity can be used with names of singers/musicians, films, food and drink, etc.

Unit 2

Grammar p.24

Oral activity

Bring in a picture of a famous person the students are familiar with (or ask a student to bring one). The students take turns to ask one another questions using the indirect form *Do you know …?*

For example:

Student 1: *Evi, do you know how old Madonna is?*

Evi: *Maybe about 40?*

To add an extra element of challenge, tell students they must not answer 'Yes' or 'No', but must make a guess.

Unit 3

Reading p.28

Lead-in (books closed)

Write the title of the reading passage on the board – All4U – and ask students the 'normal' way of writing it. Then ask if they know any similar expressions (these are often used by young people when sending text messages), e.g. CU = see you, 2day = today, U R Gr8 = You are great.

Grammar p.30

Game

Write the following people on the board

your teacher   the head of your school

a film star you admire   a five-year-old child

a shop assistant   the waiter in a café

your mother or father   a very old woman in the street

a policeman   a small puppy   the leader of your country

Students work in teams and think of a request they might make to each of them.

They write down their requests and then read them out to the class in jumbled order. The rest of the class has to guess

who each request is addressed to.

For example:

I wonder if I could have your autograph? (request to a film star)

Points can be given for each correct guess and/or for each correctly formed request.

Unit 4

Reading p.36

Lead-in

Students write down the names of three people in their family. They discuss with a partner whether each person does any sport, and if so, what. If they don't, what type of sport might be suitable?

Follow-up

Students discuss which sports activity they'd like to do or wouldn't like to do. Which of these sports might be suitable for the other family members they discussed earlier?

Grammar p.40

Personalised activity

Students work in pairs and discuss things they could and couldn't do three years ago. They must find three things they could both do at that time, three things neither of them could do, one thing student A could do but not student B, and one thing that student B could do but not student A.

Unit 5

Reading p.42

Lead-in

Ask students to tell you which restaurants in the region they like going to and why.

Grammar p.46

Oral activity

Ask students to work in groups and find out the places where their clothes or possessions were made. (They may need to look at the labels!) For example, *Alan's jacket was made in Thailand.* The group with the biggest number of different countries is the winner.

(Alternatively, you could do this as a whole-class activity and see how many different countries can be found.)

Reading p.48

Lead-in

Ask students to work in groups and make a list of all the fruits that don't grow in their country. The group with the longest list is the winner. (If this is too difficult, put a list of fruits on the board and see if they can decide which ones are grown locally, e.g. apples, bananas, mangoes, oranges, strawberries, kiwi fruit, dates.)

Unit 6

Grammar p.53

Personalised activity

Write the name of each student on a slip of paper and give

them out in jumbled order (or get the class to do this). Ask students to write a conditional sentence about the person whose name is on the paper beginning:

If .... had lots of money, he'd/she'd ....
or *If .... could go anywhere, he'd/she'd go to ....*
or *If .... could meet any film star, he'd/she'd ....*
The students then take turns to read out their sentences and the named person says whether or not the sentence is true.

Reading p.55

Lead-in (books closed)
Choose six words from the text, e.g. *biscuits, wrapped, presents, toys, paper, expensive.*

Write them in a circle on the board. Ask students to make as many different sentences as possible using two or three of the words, e.g. *Toys are good presents for children.* Repeat until seven or eight sentences have been made (the same words can be used more than once). This will get the students thinking about the meanings of the words and how they can be combined.

Then ask the class to think of two connected sentences using all the words. Write these on the board. Tell students to open their books and read the text. Is the meaning similar, or completely different?

Unit 7

Grammar p.61

Personalised activity
Each student makes up a question beginning *Have you ever ...* . The students interview one another to find out how many people say 'yes' to their question.

Reading p.64

Lead-in (books closed)
Find out what students know about New Zealand. For example, is it nearer the North Pole or the South Pole? (South Pole) Which is the nearest continent? (Australia) What language do most people speak? (English) What are the original inhabitants called? (Maoris) What do tourists go there for? (beautiful scenery, extreme sports) What sport was invented there? (bungee jumping)

Unit 8

Reading p.68

Lead-in
Think of a place in your country a long way away from the students' town, and very different. Tell the class to imagine that their family is moving to this place, and they have to go to school there. How would they feel? What would the advantages and disadvantages be?

Grammar p.69

Personalised activity
Ask half the students to work in groups to make a list of the things they have to do and can't do at school. The other half make a similar list, but for their 'ideal' school. They show the lists to each other and discuss the differences.

Unit 9

Reading p.76

Lead-in
Ask students what they like to do in the country. How about their parents? Their grandparents? Very young children?

Grammar p.80

Oral activities
Ask students to remember as many things as possible that different people have said in the lesson so far (or in yesterday's lesson) and to report what was said,
e.g. *You told us to do Exercise 4 for homework.*

Ask students to think of three things someone said which they were glad to hear in the last 24 hours, and to report them, e.g. *My mother said we were going to have pizza tonight.*

Unit 10

Reading p.85

Follow-up
Discuss any similar museums in the students' region. Do they ever go there? Why/Why not? What might make museums more fun to go to? What special sorts of museums would they like to visit? What everyday objects of today might be in a museum in the future?

Unit 11

Grammar p.94

Personalised activity
Ask each student to write down three things they had done by the time they were ten years old. Then – in groups or as a class – the students try to find something they'd done by that age, that no-one else had done. For example, *By the time she was ten, Tina had broken her arm twice.*

Unit 12

Listening p.99

Lead-in
Ask students to brainstorm some words connected with vampires, e.g. *blood, night, bat, fly.* Have they seen any films or TV programmes about vampires? What do they think of them?

Ask what they know about the story of Dracula. (He was a vampire. He could turn other people into vampires by biting them and drinking their blood.)

Answer key and tapescripts

UNIT 1

Reading p.8

1 A

2 A

3 B (he was born in London but then moved to Manchester)

4 B (he used to share but has his own room now)

5 B (his parents moved to England after they got married)

6 A (Joe is 16, his brother is two years younger, his sister is 11)

7 B (they live in a farmhouse near Rome)

8 A ([Jas] *is brilliant at science*)

9 A (*we're looking for another guitarist*)

10 B (next year they'll be split up)

Speaking p.10

1 1 Where do you live?

2 How long have you lived there?

3 Do you like living there?

4 Tell me about your parents.

5 How many brothers and sisters have you got?

6 What do you do?

7 What are your hobbies?

8 What do you like doing in the evenings?

9 How long have you studied English?

10 Do you enjoy studying English?

2 1   a) 2   b) 3   c) 5   d) 6   e) 10

3 London   teacher   brother   hobbies   study   hospital

Vocabulary p.11

1 1 I have three **brothers** (two older and one younger) and one younger **sister** so I always have someone to talk to. My **mother** and **father** both come from large families and so I have many **uncles**, **aunts** and **cousins** …

2 1 schoolfriend   2 grandmother   3 sister
   4 neighbours   5 boyfriend   6 cousins

2 1 altogether (*altogether* – used with a total number; *all together* = in the same place)

2 some times (*there are (some) times when* … – here *times* is a plural noun; *sometimes* is an adverb like *always* and *never* – it tells us 'how often')

3 all ready (*all ready* = completely ready; *already* = before now)

4 every day (*every day* is written as two words)

3 1 sister   2 seaside   3 family   4 friends   5 chocolate
   6 apple   7 cleaning

Reading p.12

1 1 the writer's grandmother

2 the writer's grandfather (a soldier)

3 in a village in the north of England

4 He was sent away to Egypt.

5 five years

6 yes (and they got married)

2 1 D   2 B   3 B   4 C   5 A   6 D   7 A   8 D   9 A
   10 C

Grammar p.13

1 1 big   2 older   3 expensive   4 up-to-date   5 cheap

2 1 highest   2 expensive   3 strongest   4 cheapest
   5 comfortable

3 1 very   2 too   3 too   4 enough

Writing p.14

1 more

2 less homework than (NOT less than)

3 older than

4 better at

5 enough money

Listening p.15

1

Example 1

missing words: seven, half, after, eight

answer: B

Example 2

missing words: long, short, glasses

answer: A

Tapescript

Example 1

B: *If you need the book, I can bring it round to your house tonight. Will you be in?*

G: *Well, I've got an English class until seven o'clock, but I'll be back about half an hour after that.*

B: *OK, that's fine. I'm meeting Richard at eight, but I can come round to your place first; it's on the way anyway.*

Example 2

W: *This is me when I was twelve. I had really long hair then. I wanted it short but my mother wouldn't let me. And look at those awful glasses. I hated them!*

M: *Oh, I think you look nice in glasses.*

2 1 A   2 C   3 C   4 A   5 B   6 B   7 B

Tapescript

1

When will the woman phone Steve?

A: *I'm afraid I don't have the information now, Steve, but I can phone you back. Will you be in this afternoon?*

B: *Well, I have to go out at about half past three for an hour or so ... so either before then, around three, or after I get back, say about five o'clock?*

A: *I'll call back before you go out if that's OK?*

B: *Fine, great.*

2

Which photograph are they looking at?

A: *That's my grandma ...*

B: *She looks really young.*

A: *Actually she's nearly 70.*

B: *Mmm, I'd never have thought she was your grandma. I suppose it's because her hair's so dark. You always imagine a grandmother with white hair, don't you?*

3

Where is Polton?

A: *Where do you come from?*

B: *Oh, just a small town ... it's called Polton.*

A: *Where is that exactly? Isn't it near Birmingham?*

B: *It's between Birmingham and Oxford, but it's actually nearer Oxford.*

4

Who lives in the apartment?

A: *Well, we have a big apartment and it's a good thing because there are quite a lot of us – my mother and father, and my grandfather. He used to live with my aunt, but now he lives with us. And there's me, of course.*

5

Where is the boy's computer now?

A: *Where's your computer?*

B: *Oh, I moved it. The light was wrong where it was. I was sitting opposite the window and the sun got in my eyes. So I've moved it out of the dining room and put it in my bedroom where the cupboard was before, next to the door, and I moved the cupboard into the dining room.*

6

What sport does Paul do now?

A: *What about sports, Paul? What's your favourite sport?*

P: *Well, I used to love football when I was younger, but I don't have time for that at present. I still like watching it on TV – but … I don't know, I do manage to go jogging sometimes, at the weekends.*

A: *You used to do quite a lot of cycling, didn't you?*

P: *Yeah, and tennis as well. I might take that up again when I have time.*

7

What is the girl's mother doing at present?

A: *What about your mother? Does she have a job?*

B: *Well, she was a nurse before she got married. Then when she had me and my sisters, she gave up work for a bit and looked after us ... but she's just started doing a course, she's studying to be a teacher.*

A: *How long will that take?*

B: *Three years. Then she'll be a qualified primary teacher. She says it's something she's always wanted to do.*

Reading p.17

1 B   2 C   3 C   4 A   5 B

Note: 1 This is a personal message. 2 This is on an official form. 3 You can find this on a bottle of tablets. 4 This is on a leaflet giving the rules for a competition. 5 You can find this in a magazine.

UNIT 2

Vocabulary p.18

1 1 kitchen   2 dining room   3 bedroom
4 bathroom   5 garage   6 hall   7 living room   8 study

Tapescript

1 Dinner won't be long – I'm just making the salad.
2 Could you put the plates on the table for me, please?
3 This room is so untidy – you haven't even made the bed!
4 I won't be long – I'm just cleaning my teeth!
5 As you can see, it's quite small but it's big enough to get the car in.
6 Can you take your boots off before you come in? It's rather wet outside.
7 I wish you'd be quiet – I can't hear the television!
8 It's nice to have a separate place where I can have my computer and all my books and papers.

2 1

1 wardrobe	bedroom
2 television	living room
3 fridge	kitchen
4 cooker	kitchen
5 shower	bathroom
6 sofa	living room
7 dining table	dining room/kitchen
8 desk	study/bedroom
9 sink	kitchen
10 coffee table	living room

2

Example answers

bedroom – bed, cupboard; living room – chair, bookshelf; kitchen – washing machine; bathroom – bath; dining room – cupboard; study – computer

3 1 pillow, cushion
2 chair, armchair
3 bed, sofa
4 light, lamp
5 heater, fire
6 carpet, mat
7 curtains, blind
8 switch, button

Writing p.19

1 2 lamp 3 alarm clock 4 storage boxes 1 CD rack 2

Tapescript

1 *They're made of plastic and you can get them in lots of different colours and sizes. I need lots of them because I'm really untidy and there aren't enough cupboards in my room. I like them because they're cheap and they help me to keep my things tidy.*

2 *It's very long and it's yellow and you can turn it round. I need it because I've got lots of CDs and I can never find the one I want. I like it because it doesn't take up much space and yellow is my favourite colour.*

3 *It's made of metal and it's silver-coloured. It's very unusual because it's got two legs and two feet, and you can move them and bend them just like real legs. I need one because I keep getting headaches when I'm working. I like it because it gives a good light and it makes me laugh because it looks funny.*

4 *It's made out of metal and it's green and gold-coloured. The face lights up at night so you can see the time. I need it because I can never wake up in the morning. I like it because it's easy to see and it makes a really loud noise.*

2 1 She bought the lamp.
2 **Description of what she bought:** 4 sentences: Yes, yesterday I bought something really nice – a new lamp for the desk in my bedroom. It's made of metal and it's silver-coloured. It's got two legs which bend just like real legs, and two feet. It's even got a name – it's called 'Mr Jim'.

Why she needed it: 2 sentences: I really needed a lamp because the light in my bedroom isn't very good. I found I kept getting a headache when I was doing my homework.

What she thinks about it: 2 sentences: Now I can see very clearly and I don't get any more headaches. And it makes me laugh because it looks funny!

Language spot p.20

a) London (name of city), English (nationality), Mrs Smith (name of person), Tuesday (name of day), July (name of month), Germany (name of country), The Sleeping Beauty (title)

b) It's an alarm clock for my bedroom. It's made of plastic and it's bright red.

Reading p.20

1 1 F (the capital is Canberra)
2 F (summer is from December to March)
3 T
4 T
5 T

2 1 A
2 B (they used to be schools in the past)
3 A
4 B (you hire them, which means they are not free)
5 B (there are only shared, twin, double and family rooms)
6 A
7 B (the rooms sleep four to ten people)
8 B (it is the second most popular hostel, not the first)
9 A
10 A

Reading p.22

1 2 b)

2 1 C 2 D 3 A 4 B 5 B 6 A 7 C 8 D 9 C
10 B

3 *Example answers*
drink hot tea in an ice cup; open a window; have a hot bath; sit by a fire; sit on an ice chair without falling off

4 1 *Example answer*

> *Dear Joe*
> *I'm staying in a hotel called the Icehotel, where*
> *everything's made of ice.*
> *I like the cinema, which has a big ice screen.*
> *However, I don't like my ice bed much because it's*
> *hard and cold.*

2 Where you are staying, what you like about it and what
you don't like.

Reading p.23

1 A   2 C

Note: 1 Advertisements for selling houses can be found in
newspapers or magazines. 2 This can be found on a leaflet or
brochure. Youth hostels are cheap places where both young
and older people can stay.

Speaking p.23

2   1c)   2e)   3a)   4d)   5b

Tapescript

*I can see a big room – it might be a room in a hostel because
there are a lot of beds. I can't see any windows. There is a
big thing in the middle of the room – it might be a table. The
beds are one on top of the other in the room so a lot of
people can sleep there. They all have white sheets and
pillows. They are … I can see a lot of bags in the room and I
can see a lot of people in the room and they're all men. They
seem quite young – they look like students and I think they
are quite fit – they are all wearing jeans and T shirts. I think
they might be feeling tired – so they could be going to bed
or they could be getting up in the morning. They might be
getting ready to go on to a different place.*

Grammar p.24

1   Well, **who is coming** then?
   Who invited Kevin?
   Which restaurant are we going to?
   Why did you choose that? It's so noisy.

Tapescript

A: *Is Peter coming with us to the restaurant tonight?*
   No, he isn't. I don't know why not.
A: *Well, who is coming then?*
B: *Oh, Susie, John and Kevin.*
A: *Who invited Kevin?*
B: *I think Susie did – she likes him.*
A: *Which restaurant are we going to?*

B: *Pizza House.*
A: *Why did you choose that? It's so noisy.*
B: *Yes, but it's cheap.*

2   1 c)   2 d)   3 b)   4 a)

3   1 are the
   2 know who is
   3 know where
   4 if/whether they are
   5 got

Listening p.25

1 B   2 C   3 A   4 B   5 C   6 A

Tapescript

*This is the Merseyside National Trust Tour Information Centre.
Unfortunately the office is closed at the moment but
information about tours follows this message. All tours are
organised by the National Trust, a charity which aims to look
after buildings of historical importance in Britain.*
Tour of 20 Forthlin Road
*The small house at 20 Forthlin Road, Liverpool was the family
home of Sir Paul McCartney of the famous group The Beatles.
The house was bought by Paul McCartney's parents in the
1950s and it was here that he and his brother Michael
McCartney grew up. The house has now been bought by The
National Trust. It is open to the public on Wednesdays and
Saturdays from April to September and on Saturdays only
from October to March.*
*A minibus to the house leaves from the Albert Docks four
times daily on these days. Members of the National Trust pay
£2.50 to cover the minibus trip. Tickets for non-members are
£5.50 for adults and £2.80 for children and as well as
transport to the house, this price includes an introductory
video which you can watch on entry to the house as well as a
recorded description of the house which you can listen to as
you walk around. There is also a small shop at the house
where souvenirs and gifts can be bought. Visitors are asked
to note that refreshments are not available at the house.*
*Visitors to the house will be able to see much of the original
furniture on the ground and first floors, together with many
photographs of John, Paul, George and Ringo in the early
days of The Beatles. During their tour visitors can listen to a
recorded account of how Paul taught himself to play the
guitar as a teenager, and can stand in the small front room
where Paul and John wrote the first Beatles hit song 'Love
Me Do'. They can also hear recordings of the songs
themselves and of friends and neighbours of The Beatles
talking about their memories.*
*Visitors are reminded that all handbags and cameras must be
left at the entrance to the house, and that they are not*

permitted to take photographs inside the house. Wheelchair users can visit most of the ground floor of the house, but will not be able to visit the bedrooms on the first floor.
Thank you for calling us and we hope you will enjoy your visit.

UNIT 3

Vocabulary p.26

1 1 2 play   3 ride   4 visit   5 go   6 go   7 read
8 watch   9 go   10 do   11 stay   12 help

2 1 1 painting a picture   2 playing the guitar
3 using a computer   4 photography   5 skiing
2 camera 4   music 2   paints 1   computer 3
brush 1   skis 5   guitar 2   mouse 3   film 4

Reading p.27

2 d)

3 1 C   2 D   3 D   4 A   5 D   6 B   7 B   8 C   9 A
10 D

Reading p.28

1 A
2 D
3 D (*their recent songs have lacked … original ideas*)
4 C (*they've started to get back their old magic*)
5 B (C is describing a song, not a CD; A and D contain incorrect information)

Reading p.29

1 A   2 B   3 C

Note: 1 This is an email. 2 You can find this in an advertisement for books that you buy by mail order. 3 You can read this in a magazine.

Grammar p.30

1 1 a) Hey, **can I** borrow that CD?
b) **Could I** borrow this CD, please?
c) **I wonder if I could** borrow your car tomorrow?
2 a) Steve, **can/will you** lend **me** a pen?
b) **Could/Would you** lend **me** a pen for a minute? I've left mine at home.
c) Excuse me. **I wonder if you could** let **me** know when we get to the High Street.

2 1 Can I sit here please?
Sure, no problem.
2 Would you lend me your dictionary, please?

I'm afraid I need it myself.
3 Excuse me, I wonder if you could tell me the time.
Of course. It's 10.30.
4 I wonder if you'd mind opening the window.
Certainly, it is rather hot in here.

3 1 borrow
2 would you/could you
3 I could
4 me know

Writing p.31

3 *Example answer*

> Dear Adam
> Thanks very much for your letter. In fact I like all sorts of music. I like some classical music, and modern singers too. I really like going to concerts when I get the chance.
>   Last week I went to a great concert. It was by the Baker Boys. They're my favourite group. Their lead singer has a very good voice. They sang all their old hits and some new ones. My favourite one was 'Never Say Goodbye'. It's quite sad, but the words and music are very original.
>   Have you heard of them? Who is your favourite singer?
> Write soon.
> Best wishes
> Paula

4 I really like Robbie Williams, in fact he's my favourite singer. Last week I saw him do a great concert on TV. There were thousands of people there and he sang some very good songs. My favourite is 'Angels'. Robbie sings a lot of old songs and also some new ones and he's a great performer.

Speaking p.32

2 a) drum and guitar   b) teddy bear   c) book
d) video   e) ball

3 1 video ✓   2 book ✗   3 teddy bear ✗

4

Tapescript

1

A: *Well, I think the video is a good idea because all children like cartoons.*

B: *Yes, and as well as that it would keep them quiet.*

A: *Yes, but on the other hand they're just sitting in front of the television all afternoon. That's not very good for them.*

2

B: *The book might be a problem because maybe the children can't read it.*

A: *No, but we could read to them. Children like listening to stories.*

B: *That's a good idea.*

3

A: *The teddy bear wouldn't be any good for the boys.*

B: *But my little brother has one and he really likes it!*

A: *But it's more for bedtime, isn't it? Not for playing with.*

5 Object   drums
     Advantage   children love making noise, will play a long time
     Disadvantage   gives me a headache, neighbours won't like it

     Object   ball
     Advantage   children can play together
     Disadvantage   they might break something

Tapescript

1

A: *I think we should use the drums – children always love making a noise and they will play for a long time.*

B: *That's true, but it will give me a headache!*

A: *And I suppose the neighbours won't like it!*

2

A: *How about a ball? They can play with each other and we needn't play with them!*

B: *But they might break something – like a window.*

A: *Yes, that's a good point.*

Listening p.33

1 Three book titles are mentioned (*Look Behind You, Just in Time, Chocolate Kisses*).

2 1 C   2 B   3 A   4 A   5 B   6 B

Tapescript

Welcome to 'Improve your English' ... and today we're going to look at reading, but not the sort you do at school in your English classes. Instead we'll be looking at some books you can read on your own at home, maybe in the evening or at weekends. In fact this sort of reading for pleasure is one of the best ways to improve your English – your vocabulary and grammar too – without even thinking about it. But the most important thing is to choose the right book. That means finding a book about something that interests you personally – if you don't like historical novels in your own language, for example, you probably won't enjoy them in English either. Now these books are specially written for students at different levels of English so you need to find the right level

for you. In fact it's a good idea to choose a book that seems a bit easy, then you can read it quickly without having to worry about looking up lots of words in the dictionary. If you choose something too difficult, you'll probably never manage to finish it.

So let's look at three of the latest books. The first one is a thriller and it's called 'Look Behind You'. It takes place in Scotland. The hero is Bruce, a computer science student. One night he sees a murder in a crowded street. But no one believes him. Then he starts getting strange messages on his computer. I won't tell you what happens next, but I promise you won't stop reading until you get to the end.

If you like science fiction, you might like to try 'Just in Time'. The heroine, Mara, is a teenager who lives in the year 2090. The population of the world is dying because there isn't enough food, and scientists send a message to outer space asking for help. But when the visitors from space arrive, they come as enemies, not friends, and only Mara knows the secret that can stop them destroying the world completely. And finally, a love story. Annie is an American girl working in a restaurant in Italy. She falls in love with Pietro, whose family owns the restaurant. But Pietro's mother's not happy about her son marrying an American. Then Annie's old schoolfriend comes on the scene, with surprising results. 'Chocolate Kisses' is an unusual love story which I'm sure you'll enjoy.

UNIT 4

Vocabulary p.34

1 1   1 football   2 high jump   3 baseball
      4 gymnastics   5 hockey   6 volleyball   7 rugby
      8 rowing

    2   1 balance (gymnastics)   2 hold (hockey)
      3 jump (high jump)   4 throw (rugby)
      5 catch (baseball)   6 kick (football)   7 hit (volleyball)
      8 row (rowing)

    3   1 football, rugby, hockey, baseball, volleyball
      2 gymnastics

2 1   1 cycling (*riding, fell off*)   2 surfing (*a big wave, fell off my board*)   3 athletics (*running on the track*)
      4 tennis (*hit me ... with her racket*)

Listening p.35

1 ankle   2 rest   3 walk (on it)   4 ice   5 eight   6 exercises

Tapescript

D: *Well now, it's Lucy, isn't it, Lucy Martin?*

L: *Mmm.*

D: *Well, Lucy, we've just had a look at the X-ray we took of*

your leg, and we can see from the X-ray picture that there are no broken bones, so that's good news, but you do have quite a badly twisted ankle. You said you fell during a gym lesson, didn't you?

L: *Yes.*

D: *You must have just fallen with your weight on the ankle. I'm afraid it's going to be quite painful for a few days, so this is what you should do. First of all, try to rest your ankle as much as you can. It's best if you don't walk on it more than you have to for the next few days. And every hour or so you should put some ice on the ankle, but don't leave it on for more than 20 minutes every hour – ice from the freezer is fine, you can even use frozen peas or something. Then later on when the ankle looks more its normal size, and the swelling has gone down, you can just put this bandage on. It's elastic, so it will just support the ankle for you. If you're in a lot of pain and you can't sleep, just take a couple of these pain killers tonight, but don't take more than eight in 24 hours. Now I'm going to make an appointment for you in seven days' time to go to Clinic 6, and they'll show you some exercises for your ankle. These will mean that you can get it working again as soon as possible. OK?*

Reading p.36

1 F (not B or H, she doesn't like swimming)

2 C (B and H are for women only)

3 A (not E as this is not a class)

4 D (not B as they don't take large groups)

5 E (not A as this is a class, not individual work; not G as no mention of qualified staff)

Speaking p.37

1 *Example answers*

  1 on a country road

  2 jogging/running

  3 shorts, T-shirt, trainers

  4 to get fit

  5 tired

Writing p.38

1 1 You have to write about three things in each task.

  2

  1

  Dear Steve

  Thanks very much for inviting me to dinner last night. I really enjoyed the meal, especially the chocolate dessert! I hope you can come round to my flat for a meal soon – how about sometime next week?

  Carlotta

2

Hi Annie

I'm sorry, but I can't go to the concert tomorrow night. I've hurt my ankle playing volleyball and I can't walk. We could ask Sam if he wants to go in my place – I'm sure he'd like to.

Best wishes

Guido

2 1 c 2 b 3 e 4 a 5 d

3 1 say what you are enjoying most

  2 *Example answer*

> Dear Adam
> Hi! I'm staying in a place called Cadgwith. It's a seaside fishing village, with lots of old houses and some good beaches nearby. I'm really enjoying the water sports, especially surfing!
> Hope to see you soon.
> All the best
> Jack

4 *Example answer*

> Jack – I'm going to see the latest Harry Potter film tonight. Would you like to come with me? If so, we could meet outside the multi-screen cinema in town at 7.00.
> Hope to see you there.
> Ahmed

Grammar p.40

1 1 Can can't can can't Can't

Tapescript

A: *We're all going swimming on Sunday. Can you come with us?*

B: *Well, I'd love to, but I can't. I've got so much homework.*

A: *You can do it on Sunday evening. Come on. It'll be fun.*

B: *Well, actually I can't swim.*

A: *Can't you? It's easy. I'll teach you. So you're coming?*

B: *OK, thanks.*

2 1 are not able to 2 are able to 3 unable/not able

2 1 correct 2 incorrect (It should be *managed to*) 3 incorrect (It should be *managed to* or *was able to*.) 4 correct 5 correct

3 1 able

  2 able to

  3 to swim

4 manage
5 able to

Reading p.41

1 A   2 C

Note: 1 This might be a temporary sign in a public place. 2 This could be found in the changing rooms of a public swimming pool.

Reading p.41

1 1 a) China   b) at least two thousand years ago

2 1 B   2 D   3 C   4 A   5 C   6 A   7 A   8 B
9 C   10 B

3 The ball was different. The game was played all over a town (not in a stadium). There were more players. There were no teams and no rules. The game could go on all day.

U N I T 5

Reading p.42

1 C   2 C

Note: 1 You could read this sign in a public building or restaurant. 2 This is an advertisement for a restaurant.

Reading p.42

1 A (All the other restaurants serve English food or are unsuitable for smokers/a large party)
2 E (vegetarian and non-vegetarian, allows smoking)
3 D (fast service, open lunchtime)
4 H (not F as they have children)
5 B (not D as it doesn't mention take away)

Vocabulary p.44

1 1 vegetables   2 drinks   3 bread   4 meat   5 fish
6 seasoning   7 fruit   8 salad

2 1 pasta, dessert
2 egg, milk
3 lettuce, meat
4 salt, vegetable
5 bread, drink

3 1 fork   2 table   3 dessert   4 waiter   5 main course
6 menu   7 drink   8 starter   9 knife   10 tip
The word is *restaurant*.

5 *Example answer*

Dear Tony

Thanks very much for your letter. I'm glad you had such a good time at the restaurant.

In my family, when we are celebrating something, we usually have a big meal at home. When it was my grandfather's 60th birthday we had a big meal for him. It was a lovely day, so we ate outside. We had salads and cold chicken, and then cheese and fruit. My mother had made a big birthday cake for him too, and we all gave him presents and sang 'Happy birthday'. I think he really enjoyed it.

Write soon.

Best wishes

Carlotta

Speaking p.45

3 1 get ready   2 bring something   3 rain   4 weather
5 expensive   6 far away   7 car   8 cheap   9 likes
10 want   11 bring some food   12 work

4 1 suppose   2 good idea   3 not   4 better   5 don't

Tapescript

A: *I think a barbecue would be really good – everyone likes barbecues.*

B: *But it's hard work …*

A: *Yes, it is. Well, a picnic's easy to get ready, and everyone can bring something. But it might rain …*

B: *Yes … so perhaps it's better if we all go to a restaurant. Then the weather doesn't matter.*

A: *I'm not sure … it might be too expensive. Why don't we get a take away? That's much cheaper.*

B: *But the take away restaurants are all too far away. You need a car.*

A: *I suppose so. We could go to a fast food restaurant and all have hamburgers – that's fun, and cheap too.*

B: *But not everyone likes that sort of food.*

A: *OK – we could just do a buffet and have it in the house. Then everyone can eat what they want.*

B: *Yes, that's a good idea – but on the other hand it's a lot of work for us.*

A: *Well, we could ask everyone to bring some food. Then we'd have less to do.*

B: *Yes, I think that's probably best.*

Grammar p.46

1 **present simple passive**: is made, are produced
past simple passive: was made, were used

2 is made by, is made by

3 1 was carried, was changed, was found

2 1 T

2 T

3 F (the milk was changed to cheese)

4 F (the cheese kept for a long time, not the milk)

5 F (some of the milk, not all of it, is still made by farmers' wives)

6 F (it is also made from goat's and sheep's milk)

7 T

4 1 c) 2 b) 3 a) 4 e) 5 d)

5 1 serves

2 is played

3 cooked

4 my coat cleaned

5 our house painted

Writing p.47

1 Time: 7.00 (not 7.30)

Menu: no vegetarian choice

Tapescript

This is the Mayfair Restaurant ringing about your booking for three people for Saturday evening. Unfortunately we have to make a change to the arrangements and we would like to ask you to come at 7.00 and not 7.30 as we have a very large party booked in for 8.30. We also regret that there will be no vegetarian choice for the main course. Please contact us on 754961 if you have any problems or questions for us. Thank you.

2 1 just 2 be 3 no 4 Do 5 could 6 about

7 Thanks

3 *Example answer*

Dear Steve
The restaurant wants us to be there at 7.00 on Saturday and there's no vegetarian choice. I'm not happy about that because I don't eat meat. Shall we go to the pizza restaurant instead? Let me know what you think.
Louise

Reading p.48

1 durian

1 what it looks like 2 what it smells like

3 what it tastes like

2 1 B 2 D 3 C 4 B 5 A 6 D 7 B 8 A 9 A

10 B

Listening p.49

1 1 a)

2 1 B (He goes there quite often.)

2 A

3 B (She's in a hurry as she has to be back at work in an hour.)

4 A

5 B (He once got ill through eating an omelette.)

6 A

Tapescript

K: *This restaurant's really nice, Peter, I don't know why I've never been here before. I've walked past it lots of times.*

P: *Oh, I come here quite often. The food's really good and it's quite reasonable. And you can usually get a place quite easily at lunchtime.*

K: *Mmm.*

P: *And it's no smoking, which I like. It really spoils my meal when people smoke in restaurants.*

K: *Me too! I'm really pleased more and more restaurants don't allow it. Anyway, I suppose we'd better have a look at the menu. I haven't got that much time as I've got to be back at work in an hour.*

P: *Sure ... now, let's see ... well, I think I'll just have the main course – I'll have the fish because I don't cook fish at home very often.*

K: *OK ... actually I'm quite hungry, so I think I'll have the beef with rice.*

P: *You really should try the fish, you know. I had it the last time I was here and I really enjoyed it. They cook it very simply, just with lemon.*

K: *I don't like fish when I'm not by the sea – I never believe it's really fresh.*

P: *I've never had a problem here.*

K: *Oh, I'm sure it's fine. But I had some bad fish once and I haven't really liked fish since then.*

P: *I know what you mean. I got ill once on holiday when I ate an omelette that had a bad egg in ... and I couldn't touch eggs for years afterwards. It really spoiled my holiday too. So you're having the beef as your main course?*

K: *Yes, and I think I'll have a starter too ... the soup looks nice.*

P: *OK then, I'll call a waiter. The service's usually quite fast here so you should be able to get back ...*

2 1 Katy 2 Peter 3 Katy 4 Katy 5 Peter

6 Peter (the fish) 7 Peter (an omelette that had a bad egg in) 8 Katy

UNIT 6

Vocabulary p.50

1 1 restaurant   2 furniture   3 soft furnishings
4 men's clothing   5 accounts   6 children's clothing
7 children's toys   8 women's clothing   9 luggage
10 accessories   11 make-up   12 lighting
13 kitchen equipment   14 electrical goods

2

socks (for Peter)	✓ third floor
lipstick	✓ ground floor
bedside lamp	✓ basement
cough medicine	✗ (chemist's)
handbag	✓ ground floor
dictionary	✗ (book shop)
apples	✗ (greengrocer's)
teddy bear	✓ second floor
tie (for grandad)	✓ third floor
sofa	✓ fourth floor
sausages	✗ (butcher's)
cushion	✓ fourth floor

3 1 A   2 C   3 A   4 B   5 A   6 C   7 B   8 B
9 C   10 A

Tapescript

1 It doesn't really fit – the sleeves are too short.
2 Have you got these boots in brown?
3 Could I have half a dozen brown rolls, please?
4 I want to order the new novel by Stephen King.
5 Can I have a bunch of those roses, please?
6 How much are the cauliflowers?
7 Can you cut me three slices of ham, please?
8 Have you got anything for earache?
9 A packet of mints and some chewing gum, please.
10 There's a really long queue at the check-out!

Speaking p.51

Part 3

2 1 F   2 F   3 T   4 T   5 T   6 F

Tapescript

1 I can see two people walking in the street.
2 There is a man and a woman and the woman is wearing a purple sweater and white trousers.
3 The woman has long dark curly hair.
4 They are looking at postcards – maybe they want to buy one.
5 They could be on holiday because they are buying postcards.
6 The man looks happy and the woman looks sad.

Part 4

1 1 incorrect (You have to talk about the kinds of shopping you don't enjoy doing as well.)   2 correct   3 incorrect

Writing p.52

1 1 in, next to   2 in, between   3 next to, on
4 in, opposite   5 in, opposite   6 in, near

2 1 opposite, office   2 really, clothes, teenagers (punctuation)   3 people, friendly   4 there, listen
5 bought, jacket   6 It's (punctuation), comfortable, expensive

3 1 The new shop **sells**   2 are   3 design**ed**
4 bought   5 It **did not cost**

4 1 1 where the shop is   2 why you like it (or don't like it)   3 something you bought there.
2 1 correct   2 incorrect   3 correct

5 *Example answer*

Dear Tom
Thanks for your letter. I really like shopping, but the shops in my town aren't very good. The best ones are in the new shopping centre in the middle of town next to the car park. There's a new clothes shop there. The people in the shop are very friendly but it is a bit expensive.
My favourite shop is called Music Central. It's a very modern shop and the things are not too expensive. Last week I bought a CD there. It didn't cost too much money because it was reduced.
I hope you'll write again soon.
Regards
Stefano

Grammar p.53

1 1 b)   2 c)   3 d)   4 a)

3 If Paul had lots of money, he'd learn to drive and buy a car.
If Annie had lots of money, she'd go to medical school and become a doctor.
If Josie had lots of money, she'd learn how to sing and become famous.
If Don had lots of money, he'd stop working and go round the world

Tapescript

I: *Paul, what would you do if you had lots of money?*
P: *What would I do if I had lots of money? I don't know really. Well, first of all I'd learn to drive. I'd really like to do that, and then I'd buy a car. That would be really cool.*

I: *Annie, what would you do if you had lots of money?*

P: *I'd go to medical school. That's my dream. Then I'd become a doctor.*

I: *Josie, what would you do if you had lots of money?*

J: *I'd learn how to sing. I really love singing and I'd become famous.*

I: *What about you, Don?*

D: *I'd stop working, and I really love travelling so I'd go round the world.*

4 1 unless   2 if   3 Unless   4 unless

5 1 unless
2 if you go
3 if/when
4 I buy
5 missed

Reading p.54

1 b)

2 1 B   2 C   3 A   4 B   5 C   6 A   7 D   8 C   9 A   10 B

Reading p.55

1 C (this tests the main ideas in the passage – it is something the woman is unhappy about)
2 A (see line 12)
3 C
4 C
5 D

Listening p.56

1 B   2 A   3 C   4 C   5 C   6 C   7 A

Tapescript

1

Where is the post office?

A: *Can you post this letter for me when you go out?*

B: *Of course – I'm going to the bank anyway and so I only have to cross the road. The post office is just opposite, on the corner. It's no problem.*

A: *Thanks.*

2

What did the man buy Sarah?

A: *I found a really good present for Sarah's birthday in the department store last week – it was a special offer. I got a blue bag and a matching umbrella for £10! They had matching gloves as well, and scarves, but they were more expensive so I didn't get them.*

B: *Anyway, she's got a blue scarf already.*

3

What is causing the traffic problem?

A: *There are problems with traffic on the M1 motorway just north of London. Traffic is moving very slowly due to a broken down lorry, and motorists are asked to avoid this area if possible.*

4

What will the man and woman have for lunch?

A: *Let's have a quick lunch – I have to go out in half an hour.*

B: *OK – what about some tomato soup? And then a cheese sandwich? I've got some sausages in the fridge but they'll take longer to cook.*

A: *Mmm ... sausages would be nice, but I really don't have time.*

5

What does the woman decide to do with her friend the next day?

A: *I was thinking of ringing Jane to see if she'd like to play tennis tomorrow.*

B: *The weather forecast isn't very good. Why don't you go to the gym instead?*

A: *Oh. I think I'll just suggest we go swimming – we can play tennis another day. I'll ring her now, before lunch.*

6

Where are the woman's car keys?

A: *I can't find my car keys and I want to go shopping. Have you seen them anywhere? I usually leave them in the hall, next to the telephone.*

B: *The last time I saw them, they were on the television in the living room.*

A: *Oh, yes, here they are. I was so sure I'd left them in the hall. Thanks.*

7

Where did the man hurt himself?

A: *I was in a hurry going downstairs, and my foot slipped. I put out my hand to save myself but I fell backwards and hit my head. I've still got a big lump there, but I'm lucky it wasn't worse. At least I didn't break anything!*

Reading p.57

1 C   2 A

Note: Both these signs can be found in shops.

UNIT 7

Vocabulary p.58

1 *Down:* sightsee explore relax travel sunbathe
Across: dance cycle
Diagonal: fish swim

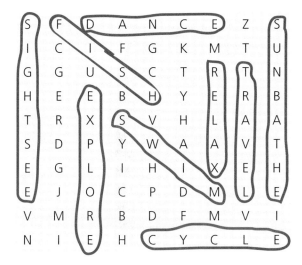

Pictures: 1 fish 2 explore 3 relax 4 travel
5 sunbathe 6 sightsee 7 swim 8 dance 9 cycle

2 1 Various answers are possible. Students should justify
their choices.

2

something to send/give to someone else	a souvenir for me to keep	something I need on holiday
postcard	T-shirt	sun-cream
necklace	picture	bottle of water
scarf		book
		guidebook
		sun hat

Tapescript

K: *It's odd – I don't like shopping much at home but I really enjoy it when I'm on holiday.*

S: *I know what you mean – it's nice going into shops and seeing different things – local things you can't get at home.*

S: *Yeah, I like choosing things for myself that will help me to remember the holiday. I buy things like pictures, and T-shirts … I've got a whole collection.*

S: *Yes, and I like buying presents for other people – you know, things like a pretty scarf or a necklace. And postcards to send to people.*

K: *And I don't even mind just the sort of ordinary shopping – for things like sun-cream and sun hats and things … even just a bottle of water. You've got lots of time, it's not like shopping at home.*

S: *Yes, and books … I like having time to look in the book shops for something to read on the beach, or a guidebook even.*

K: *Yes …*

Listening p.59

1 1 b)
2 1 a) 2 b) 3 a) 4 a) 5 b) 6a)
3 1 language classes 2 outdoor 3 cinema (trips)
4 beach party 5 950 6 registration

3 *Example answer*

> Dear Sir
> I am a 14-year-old student from Spain. I'm interested in the Adventure Course because I'd like to improve my English on holiday. Could you tell me about the accommodation – do we have to share rooms?
> Thank you.
> Ana Campella

Tapescript

A: *Hello, this is Foxton English. I believe you rang earlier to ask for information about our English Adventure Course?*

B: *Yes, that's right. Can you tell me something about it?*

A: *Well it's a very popular course, and it's partly a language course and partly an adventure holiday. So in the morning, the students have language classes and they also do projects – things like making a class magazine or producing a play. Then in the afternoon what makes this course different is that the students get out of the classroom and they have outdoor activities – things like horse-riding, mountain climbing and so on – there's a big choice. They're still using English, but they're learning something else as well. And in the evenings there's also lots for them to do … there's discos, karaoke, cinema trips and so on – there's something different every evening. Then every weekend there's a choice of three adventure trips and students can choose between the Lake District Adventure – that involves lots of climbing and hill walking – or a beach party. That's very popular, they spend the weekend camping on the beach with swimming and fishing and a campfire. And the third choice is The London Experience – that's two days in London taking in all the main tourist attractions.*

B: *And the dates?*

The dates? There is a three-week course which runs from 12–30 June, and that costs £1,425 – we have just a few places left on that – and then there's a two-week course from 13–26 August ... let's see, that's £950. That includes everything – food, all the trips and so on. If you want to book a course, please get in touch with our registration department, but if you want any more information, why don't you look at our website? The address is www.foxtonenglish.com.

B: *Great. Thanks very much.*

A: *Thank you very much, goodbye.*

Writing p.60

1 1, 3, 4, 5

Tapescript

S: *Hi, Dad.*

D: *Sam …. how are you? Enjoying yourself?*

S: *Yeah, it's great. We've been climbing – up in the rocks.*

D: *I hope you were careful!*

S: *Oh yes. I was a bit scared at first ... it was quite high … but we were all roped together, so it was quite safe. And they showed us how. It was good when we got to the top. You could see for miles.*

D: *Mmm, and what else have you done?*

S: *We've been canoeing … we did that yesterday, we went out on the sea. It was cold at first but you soon got warm, it was hard work. Then afterwards when we got back we made a fire on the beach and we had a picnic at night round the fire. It was great.*

D: *And what are the other people like?*

S: *Well, it was a bit strange at first because I didn't know anyone, but I've made some friends. There are four of us in every tent and last night we were talking all night … but I think I'll sleep tonight.*

D: *Well, I'm glad you're OK. Do you want to talk to …*

2 2 a) I had a good time too – I went on an <u>adventure</u> holiday.

b) I was a bit <u>frightened</u> because it was very high, but we had ropes and the instructor <u>helped</u> us.

c) <u>Thanks</u> for <u>your</u> letter.

d) It was <u>a</u> great <u>holiday</u>!

e) The first day we went canoeing in the <u>sea</u> and then we had a fire on the beach and a <u>picnic</u>.

f) At first I felt <u>nervous</u> because I didn't know anyone, but I soon <u>made</u> some friends.

g) The best thing <u>was</u> rock <u>climbing</u>.

h) I'm glad you <u>enjoyed</u> your <u>holiday</u>.

i) I was in <u>a</u> tent with three other <u>people</u>.

3

Dear Ken

Thanks for your letter. I'm glad you enjoyed your holiday. I had a good time too – I went on an adventure holiday. At first I felt nervous because I didn't know anyone, but I soon made some friends. I was in a tent with three other people. The first day we went canoeing in the sea and then we had a fire on the beach and a picnic. The best thing was rock climbing. I was a bit frightened because it was very high, but we had ropes and the instructor helped us. It was a great holiday!

Best wishes

Sam

Grammar p.61

1 1 **Have** you ever seen a tiger? d) Yes I **have**, but only in a zoo. I**'ve** never seen one in the wild.

2 **Has** Carla finished her homework yet? f) No, she **has**n't even started it!

3 How long **have** Helen and Kate been at this school? b) They**'ve** been here for three years.

4 **Has** anyone in your family ever been to New York? a) No, but my brother**'s** been to California.

5 **Has** Dave had that cough long? e) Yes, he**'s** had it since the beginning of last week.

6 Where **have** you put my football things? c) I**'ve** just put them in the washing machine. Do you need them now?

Tapescript

1

A: *Have you ever seen a tiger?*

B: *Yes I have, but only in a zoo. I've never seen one in the wild.*

2

A: *Has Carla finished her homework yet?*

B: *No, she hasn't even started it!*

3

A: *How long have Helen and Kate been at this school?*

B: *They've been here for three years.*

4

A: *Has anyone in your family ever been to New York?*

B: *No, but my brother's been to California.*

5

A: *Has Dave had that cough long?*

B: *Yes, he's had it since the beginning of last week.*

6

A: *Where have you put my football things?*

B: *I've just put them in the washing machine. Do you need them now?*

2

Use	Example	Time words
a) experiences in the past (we're not interested in the details)	1 and 4	Have you **ever** been? No, I've **never** been.
b) things which happened in the past (usually recently) where we are interested in the result now	2 and 6	Have you been **yet**? I've **just** been. I've **already** been.
c) things which began in the past and are still true now	3 and 5	… **since** four o'clock … **for** four years

3 1 This is the first time that I've **ever** stayed up all night.
2 I've been here **since** six o'clock. Where on earth have you been?
3 'Why are you looking so happy?' 'I've **just** heard I've passed my exam!'
4 She's **never** eaten fish in her life and I don't think she'll start now.
5 I've been living in this town **for** ten years.'
6 'Hasn't that programme finished **yet**? It's time you did your homework.' 'I've **already** done it! I did it as soon as I got home.'

4 1 a) I've worked here for a year. b) I started this job a year ago.
2 a) I've known her for years. b) I met her years ago.
3 a) She's still here. b) She hasn't left yet.
4 a) I've been there before. b) I went there a week ago.

5 1 been on holiday
2 still
3 just
4 Jaime has
5 finished

Speaking p.63

3 1 Do you agree?   2 How about you?
3 What do you think?

Reading p.64

1 1 H (not C as she has no time for a bungee jump)
2 F (not E: no old way of life; not G: no animals)
3 B (not H: B would give a better view of the city)

4 G (not D as it doesn't mention food and entertainment)
5 A (not B or C as she doesn't like heights)

3 *Example answer*

Dear Simon,
I'm having a fantastic holiday in New Zealand. I've been diving in the Tutukaka Islands and yesterday I even did a bungee jump! It was great! This afternoon I'm going to buy some souvenirs at Victoria Market. See you soon.
Love
Carla

Reading p.65

1 b)

2 1 B   2 D   3 A   4 B   5 C   6 A   7 D   8 D
9 B   10 D

3 she was wearing a thick skirt.

4 1 Skiers wear waterproof clothes because they might fall in the snow.
2 Hikers wear boots because normal shoes would hurt.
3 Mechanics wear overalls because their clothes might get dirty.
4 Police officers wear a uniform because people need to recognise them.
5 Space explorers wear space suits because they need to have air to breathe.
6 Business executives wear formal clothes because they need to look smart.

Writing p.66

1 Where/When did the story begin? – one day last holidays
What happened first? – I decided to go exploring.
What was the problem? – I got lost.

2 The best ending is C because it is surprising and we are not sure what will happen until the end. There is a strong statement at the end (*it saved my life*).
A is not good because there are too many events and not enough description. B is better, but again there is not enough description and the last sentence is not a strong ending.

Reading p.67

1 1 d)   2 a)   3 e)

2 1 A   2 A   3 B

Note: 1 You would see this at the entrance to a nightclub. 2 This is a hotel notice. 3 You would see this at a youth hostel or holiday camp.

UNIT 8

Vocabulary p.68

2 book: author, pages, title
computer: CDs, keyboard. mouse, screen
pencil case: glue, highlighters, pencils, pens, rubber, ruler, scissors

3 Susan: computer   Keith: book   Pat: friend

Tapescript

K: *What way of studying do you think's best, Susan?*

S: *I like the feel of a keyboard and the colours on the screen. I don't like books – they're boring. I much prefer to use a computer. What about you, Keith?*

K: *I don't like sitting at a table – I like to move around, or lie on my bed to study. I can't do that with a computer, so I'd much rather have a book. It's more convenient. What do you think, Pat?*

P: *think it's much better to work with another person – it's friendly and you get more ideas. So I like studying with a friend, then we can talk about our work.*

Reading p.68

1 1 D (the main focus is description – the difficult situation was her whole change in lifestyle)
2 C (she means the house and the scenery)
3 B (*I talk to Mum and she helps me see things aren't so bad*)
4 A (*I couldn't believe how much space there was*)
5 C (this is the most general answer)

3 *Example answer*

> Dear Fred
> Hi, how's life? I'm well but I really miss you all. The teachers here are fine, and the school's got a great computer centre. I've made two good friends in the computer club. Keep in touch.
> Best wishes
> Pietro

Grammar p.69

1 1 Tim's **got to** wear brown trousers at school.
2 As well as that, he **has to** wear a white shirt and a brown tie.
3 There's also a rule that all the boys **must** wear brown jackets and brown shoes.

3 1 have
2 have to

3 we have
4 aren't
5 got

Reading p.70

1 c)

2 1 C   2 D   3 D   4 A   5 A   6 D   7 B   8 D   9 C
10 A

Writing p.71

1 In my school there <u>are</u> thirty pupils in each class. We don<u>'t</u> have lunch in school because the school day finish<u>es</u> at lunchtime. <u>E</u>very afternoon we do homework or sometimes I <u>play</u> football with my friends<u>.</u> I think we have too <u>much</u> homework to do every day.

2 1 My school is quite big and modern **and** it has about 1,000 students.
2 It is a state school **so** we don't have to pay to attend classes.
3 We can do sport after school if we want to, **but** we don't have to – so I don't!
4 We can either leave school at 16 **or** we can stay until we are 18.

3 *Example answer*

> Dear Katy
> I'm really glad you're coming to stay and I hope you'll enjoy coming to school with me. My school's quite big. There are about 1,000 students there, from 13 to 18. We start lessons at 9.00 and finish at 2.00. But we don't have lunch at school. We come home for lunch, then we do our homework or go out. We have to work quite hard at school and the teachers are quite strict because they want to help us pass our exams. I hope you'll like my school and I'm looking forward to introducing you to my friends and teachers – especially my English teacher!
> See you soon.
> Best wishes
> Maria

Speaking p.72

1 1 books   lamp   bookcase   posters   4 See tapescript.

3 *Example answer*
Sally – can you meet me in the library in the quiet study room tomorrow? It would be really good if we could meet at 10.30, because I want to study grammar with you before our test.
Pat

Tapescript

*I **can see** a girl sitting on a bed. She's **studying**. She's in her bedroom. I can see a **bookcase** next to the bed and some **posters** on the wall. There are **some books** on the bed. Maybe she likes studying there because it's **quiet**, and she's got everything she needs. One problem might be that it's a bit too **comfortable**.*

*She might be feeling **tired** and maybe she'd like to **go to sleep**. Or she could be feeling quite **happy**.*

Reading p.74

1 C   2 B

Note: 1 You would see this at the entrance to a museum. 2 You would see this in a newspaper or magazine.

Listening p.74

1 a) Jim   b) unhappy (no good; needs more lessons; is worried)

2 1 B (no-one was hurt)

2 B (not mentioned)

3 A

4 A

5 B (he's worried about damaging her car)

6 B (she offers, but Jim says he'll do it)

Tapescript

κ: *Coming for a coffee, Jim?*

J: *I've got a driving lesson.*

κ: *Oh, how are they going? Booked your test yet?*

J: *No ...*

κ: *But you've been learning quite a time, haven't you?*

J: *Yes ... I just get really nervous once I'm behind the wheel. I think it's because I was in a car crash once, when I was a child ...*

κ: *Mmmm.*

J: *I was really scared ... luckily no-one was hurt, but I've never forgotten it. And anyway, I'm not all that keen on my driving teacher actually ...*

κ: *Oh?*

J: *He's just not all that good. He goes on and on talking when I'm trying to concentrate.*

κ: *What, instructions and things?*

J: *Well, sometimes, but usually stuff that's nothing to do with driving. But it must be an awful job, stuck in a car all day with hopeless drivers like me ...*

κ: *You wouldn't be hopeless with a decent teacher. The one I had, she just sat there in the passenger seat, she hardly said anything – but when she did, you listened.*

J: *Anyway, I've paid in advance and I've still got ten hours. So I'm stuck with him now. And hopefully I'll be ready to take my test then ... but I honestly don't think so.*

κ: *Well, what about if I went out with you? I mean, we could just find a quiet road somewhere and drive around ...*

J: *Yes, but I haven't got a car.*

κ: *We could use mine.*

J: *Honestly, Kate, that's really nice of you, but I'd feel awful if I did anything to it. I wouldn't be able to relax at all.*

κ: *That's a point. Well, you should do something. You could tell them you want to change teachers.*

J: *But how am I going to tell him?*

κ: *You don't have to. Just ring up the driving school. Go on, I'll do it if you don't want to.*

J: *Yes ... well, maybe ... .OK, I'll ring them.*

κ: *Do it!*

UNIT 9

Vocabulary p.75

1

Tapescript

Well, there are two hills, and there's a river ... a small river, maybe a stream which comes out from the valley between the hills and runs down to the bottom left of the picture. Just behind the stream, on the left side of the picture, there's a little cottage. It's on the side of the hill, quite near the stream. It's got a door in the middle and a window on each side of the door. Oh, and there's a chimney with smoke coming out. OK, now there's a path that goes from the front door of the cottage down towards the stream. And when it gets to the stream, it goes over a little bridge. You can't see where it goes after that because that's the bottom of the picture. And behind the cottage, on the side of the hill, there are three trees. Now, let's look at the other hill, on the right hand side of the stream. There's just one tree on this hill, and under the tree there are two sheep. Right, and now up in the sky there are two small clouds and last of all there's the sun – you can only see half of the sun because it's going down behind the hill on the right of the picture. And that's all there is in the picture. I really like it – it's all very peaceful.

2 1 A (you can't *see* nature – it's an abstract term)

2 B (in a 'tour *of* a region' you travel around for several days; in a 'trip *to* a place' you go there for a short visit, then return)

3 B (*remind* + object + infinitive; *remember* + infinitive)

4 B (*in my* can only be used with *opinion*; *idea* also suggests something original, that no-one has thought of before)

5 A (*ground* is outside; a *floor* is part of a building)

6 B (you usually *put on* clothes in the morning, when you get dressed; for the rest of the time, you are *wearing* clothes)

3 1 Susie lives in the **country**.

She lives in an **old farmhouse** with a **big garden**.

She likes it because the people are **(so) friendly** and she can go **horse-riding**.

She doesn't want to live in **London** because it's **(too) crowded and noisy**.

2 James lives in the **city**.

He lives in a **flat**.

He likes being near the **shops** and **nightlife**.

He doesn't want to live in the **country** because it's **boring**.

Tapescript

s: *Well, I quite like living in the country actually. We live in an old farmhouse and there's lots of room for all of us, and we've got a big garden. I've always lived here and I like it because everyone's so friendly and I can go horse-riding, which is what I like doing more than anything else. I'd hate to live in London or somewhere like that because it's just too crowded and noisy.*

j: *I was born here in the city and that's where I want to stay. I can't imagine living in the country. I live in a flat with my parents. It's not very big, but it's very central so it's really easy to get around. It's great to be near all the shops and the nightlife. I'd hate living in the country – it must be really boring.*

Reading p.76

1 G (not E or F as these don't mention **small** animals)

2 H (C doesn't sound exciting; D is about history; B, E and F involve animals)

3 E (this lasts the whole day and sounds exciting)

4 F (not B as this doesn't mention riding the horses)

5 A (they will not get wet as it is underground)

Speaking p.77

2 1 h)   2 g)   3 c)   4 e)   5 i)   6 b)   7 d)   8 j)   9 f)   10 a)

Tapescript

L: *I'd like to go horse-riding – I've never done it and I've always wanted to try. Can you ride?*

M: *I've never tried, but I'm not all that keen on it. It looks quite difficult – and it's a long way to fall. You could hurt yourself quite badly. Don't you think so?*

L: *Well, I'm not sure. But all right – if you don't want to do that, how do you feel about walking? That's not dangerous.*

M: *That's true. And it's good exercise – it's supposed to be really good for you. But don't you need special boots if you're walking far? I've only got these shoes, and they're not really strong enough, are they?*

L: *No. Well, you could borrow my brother's boots. I think he's got some.*

M: *I don't know if that would work. I've got really big feet. They might not be very comfortable. How about just going for a picnic? We could put some food in the car and find a nice place.*

L: *Well, I'm not sure. You mean just drive around in the car and then sit and eat?*

M: *Yes. I think it would be nice. We could just relax.*

L: *But actually I'd rather get some exercise.*

M: *Oh, OK.*

Listening p.78

1 A

2 A

3 B (he says he didn't know what was going on)

4 B (she says they all seemed the same and she didn't care what happened to them)

5 A

6 B (it said it would be bright and sunny with some clouds later)

Tapescript

N: *What did you think of the film?*

J: *I don't know … I usually like action movies, but I'm not so sure about this one.*

N: *Well it certainly wasn't boring … not at the end anyway. There was so much action!*

J: *The last part was great, yes. That final scene with the fishing boat in the storm …*

N: *Yeah, you felt as if you were right in the middle of it – as if one of the waves was going to crash down on top of you.*

J: *I know, that really big wave at the end ... that was good.*

N: *Mmm. But apart from that bit, I didn't find it all that believable.*

J: *No I didn't like the first part much. It wasn't until about three quarters of the way through the film that anything actually happened. In fact, I nearly fell asleep once near the beginning.*

N: *Yes, I noticed. But I agree, yes. And the first scenes, with the fishermen on shore and all their relationships with one another – who liked who and who didn't ... I didn't know what was going on at all.*

J: *I know it was supposed to be a true story, but I think the people all seemed the same, and to be honest, I didn't really care what happened to them.*

N: *And I kept thinking, you know, these fishermen, we were meant to feel sorry for them when the storm came, but actually fishermen nowadays, they have all sorts of special weather forecast information. Why didn't they just listen to the radio or something? Then they'd never have gone out to sea ...*

J: *Yes, they could have saved themselves a whole load of trouble!*

N: *Well, look at today's forecast – did you see it on the television this morning? Bright and sunny, with some clouds later in the day.*

J: *Huh. Well, it's not actually raining yet, but I'm glad I brought my umbrella, all the same.*

Writing p.78

Example answer

The weather forecast had said it was going to be a bright, sunny day. So Adam and I decided to sail to the island just off the coast. By eleven o'clock we were there. 'Isn't it perfect?' said Adam. 'We've got the whole island to ourselves.' We swam and fished, but then it suddenly started to get cold. We realised there was a big storm coming and set off back to land. Half way back the boat sank, but a big wave picked us up and threw us onto the beach. We were lucky to be alive. But after that I was always frightened of what the sea could do.

Reading p.79

1 b)

2 1 D   2 B   3 C   4 C   5 A   6 A   7 D   8 B   9 C   10 A

4 *Example answer*

Sorry – I think we'll have to cancel the picnic today as the weather is so bad. What do you think about having the picnic next Tuesday instead? We could go to the park then. Let me know what you think.

Grammar p.80

1 1 c); that she hoped, that day
2 a); that she was, them the next day
3 d); that she had been, the week before
4 b); that she had stayed, there

2 1 e); wanted
2 c); to
3 a); if, could
4 f); me not
5 b); told, to
6 d); she could

3 1 She said, 'I am hoping to arrive in the evening.'
2 'Where do you live?' she asked.
3 'I never expected to see you here,' he said.
4 'Why not?' she asked.
5 'Stop here!' he ordered them.
6 They said they had had a long journey.

4 1 want
2 We saw
3 Can I
4 Don't
5 We have/They have

Reading p.81

1 C   2 A

Note: 1 This could be a notice in a park.   2 You would find this notice in a country area.

UNIT 10

Vocabulary p.82

1 No fixed answers. Students should give reasons for their own answers.

2 1 pilot, doctor   2 disk jockey, dentist   3 engineer, hairdresser   4 secretary, scientist   5 firefighter, police officer

3 1 A firefighter *puts out fires.*
2 A pilot *flies planes.*
3 A doctor *looks after people's health.*
4 An engineer *builds bridges or repairs machinery.*
5 A police officer *makes sure people follow the law.*
6 A dentist *looks after your teeth.*
7 A disk jockey *plays records in clubs and discos.*
8 A scientist *does experiments in a laboratory.*
9 A hairdresser *washes and cuts your hair.*
10 A secretary *types letters and answers the telephone.*

4 1 receptionist   2 patients   3 instructor   4 assistant
5 housewife   6 criminals   7 detective
8 businessman

Reading p.84

1 a)

2 1 C   2 C   3 A   4 B   5 B   6 A   7 C   8 D
9 D   10 B

Language spot p.84

a) 1 to work   2 performing   3 studying   4 to be
5 to make   6 to let
b), d) Verbs followed by *-ing*: enjoy, finish + avoid, keep
Verbs followed by infinitive: want, hope, expect, refuse + decide, manage

Reading p.85

2 1 A
2 B (lace was made **by hand** in the villages)
3 A
4 B (the people who work the machines have over 150 years' experience)
5 B (it is a whole area of the city)
6 A
7 A
8 A
9 B (it is near the city centre car parks)
10 B (you can walk from the station)

Listening p.86

1 1 musical   2 factory workers   3 1 metre 60
4 sing   5 August   6 the town hall

Tapescript

And now, here's a chance for any of you who think you may be undiscovered actors. Capital Films are looking for young people to take part in scenes in their new film. You don't need to have any experience, but it'll be lots of fun. It's a musical, so there'll be lots of singing and dancing, and it's called 'Victoria'! It's about the early life of the girl who became Queen at the age of 18 at a time when the industrial revolution was changing the face of England forever. Capital Films are looking for about 50 young people – boys and girls – to play factory workers. At that time children as young as six or seven used to work in the factories looking after the machines. Now they don't want anyone that young, but if you're between the age of 11 and 16, and not more than 1 metre 60 tall, Capital Films would like to hear from you. Now, they're also looking for three or four boys for slightly larger parts, and for these they're looking for boys who can sing, so if you've got a good voice, why not go for it? Whether you want one of these bigger parts or just a smaller one, you need to be available for the first two weeks in August. You'll be paid a daily fee and you'll have the chance to work with the stars.
So if you'd like to know more, just come along round to the town hall at 10.00 this Saturday and who knows, you could end up a film star yourself!
And now for something ...

2 *Example answers*
pay, hours of work, number of days, what they have to do, whether you have to provide anything, e.g. costume, whether you have to sing or dance

Grammar p.86

1 1 b)   2 c)   3 a)

2 1 so that he can / in order to   2 so that he can / in order to

3 1, 2 Although / While (either order)
3, 4 although / but (either order)

4 1 The office was so cold that I got ill.
It was such a cold office that I got ill.
2 The computers were so old that they were always breaking down.
They were such old computers that they were always breaking down.
3 The weather was so bad that I couldn't stay outside.
It was such bad weather that I couldn't stay outside.

4 It was so sunny that I couldn't see my computer screen.
It was such a sunny day that I couldn't see my computer screen.

5 1 so that
2 but/although/though
3 as/because/since
4 such a useful
5 much travelling

Writing p.88

Example answer

Dear Chris
Thanks for your letter. You asked about the job I'd like.
Well, I'd like to be a professional football player. I've
always loved football. My father always encouraged me
to play, and he used to take me to matches. If I was a
professional player, I'd travel around the country and
even to other countries. Footballers get really good
pay so I'd live in a big house and drive a fast car! But
I'm afraid it's never likely to happen – I'm not even in
the school team!
Hope to see you soon.
Best wishes

Reading p.88

1 1 Dogs are not allowed in the shop.
2 In case of fire, leave by the nearest exit.
3 Please do not take towels from your room to beach.
4 Please use other door until next week when reception re-opens.
5 Films rented on Friday must be returned on Sunday.
6 We accept all types of credit cards in this shop.
7 Children under 15 are not allowed to rent this film.
8 Smoking is not allowed anywhere in the building.
9 No parking – private road.
10 Private property. No entry.

2 a) 1, 5, 6, 7
b) 2, 3, 4, 8
c) 9, 10

3 a) <u>You must not smoke</u> anywhere in the building. 8
b) <u>You can use</u> all types of credit cards in this shop. 6
c) <u>You are not allowed to park</u> your car at <u>any time</u> <u>because the</u> road <u>is</u> private <u>property</u>. 9
d) <u>You can't</u> rent this film <u>if you are</u> under 15. 7
e) <u>You are not allowed to enter at any time because this is</u> <u>a</u> private <u>place</u>. 10

f) <u>You must</u> use <u>the</u> other door until next week <u>as</u> reception <u>is closed now</u>. 4
g) <u>If you rent a film</u> on Friday <u>then you have to return it</u> on Sunday. 5
h) <u>You should</u> not take <u>the</u> towels from your room to <u>the</u> beach. 3
i) <u>If there is</u> a fire, <u>you must</u> leave <u>using</u> the nearest exit. 2
j) <u>You must</u> not <u>bring</u> dogs <u>into</u> the shop. 1

4 1 b) *You must* stand behind *the* red line when *you are* waiting for service.
2 d) You *must / should / can / may* apply for *the* job on *the* enclosed form.
3 a) You *must / should* only use this in emergencies.
4 e) You *must not* run in *the* corridor.
5 c) *I will* meet you at six. You *must not* be late!

5 1 A   2 C

Note: 1 You would find this notice in a shop.   2 You would find this notice in a public building.

U N I T **11**

Vocabulary p.90

1

Across: tower block, shop, market, park, cinema, hospital
Down: restaurant, taxi rank, library, bank, cathedral, bus station
Diagonal: café, theatre, disco, bar

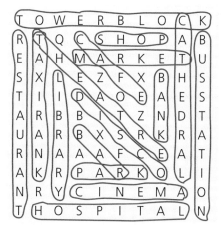

2 1 1 market   2 cathedral   3 bar   4 shop   5 cinema
6 bus station   7 tower block   8 bank   9 restaurant
10 taxi rank   11 library   12 theatre   13 disco
14 park   15 café   16 hospital

Tapescript

In the middle of the city there's a square, and in the square there's a market. On the north side of the square there's a cathedral, and on the east side there's a bar with a shop next to it. Next to the shop there's a road with a cinema on one side and a bus station opposite it. Beyond the bus station, in the distance, there is a tower block.

On the side of the square opposite the cathedral there's a bank, and next to it there is a restaurant. There's another road going from the north-west corner of the square with a taxi rank on one side and a library next to it. On the other side of the road there's a theatre and beside the theatre there's a disco. This road goes past a park, which has got a café inside, and on the other side of the park, behind the cathedral, there's a hospital.

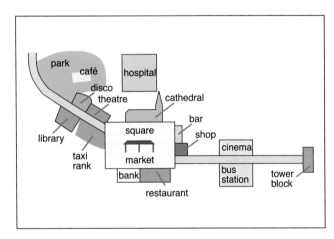

3 1 Speaker 1 A   Speaker 2 B   Speaker 3 A
Speaker 4 C
2 dangerous dirty exciting expensive fun
lively stressful

Tapescript

A: *I love it – it's really exciting living here. There's always something to do, you never get bored.*

B: *It's dirty, and there's so much traffic, it's quite dangerous for the children. I find it really stressful.*
I wish we could live in the country.

C: *All my friends live here. There are cinemas, theatres, shops. It's just fun to be here. It's the only place to live, really.*

D: *Well, there are good and bad sides to living in the city. I like having all the shops around, and it's very lively, but it's a bit expensive to live here really.*

Reading p.92

2 1 C (this text is a sort of advertisement from the owners of Eatwell Restaurants, showing how they are helping to reduce litter)
2 A (*in Singapore you can be sent to prison for it*)
3 B (*we are all responsible for this problem*)
4 D (*we provide … public litter bins*)
5 B (the text is about how Eatwell Restaurants try to reduce litter *in any town … in which we operate*;
C is too general)

Reading p.93

1 b)

2 1 C   2 D   3 D   4 C   5 C   6 B   7 D   8 D   9 A
10 B

Grammar p.94

1 had lived, hadn't learned, Had he enjoyed

3 1 [1] I did not do anything [2] until I had received his letter.
2 [1] I had just finished my homework [2] when the phone rang.
3 [1] As soon as I had had breakfast, [2] I left the house.
4 [2] Before I had even opened the door, [1] I knew who was there.
5 [2] I understood everything [1] after I had read his letter.
6 [1] After I had had my lunch, [2] I had a short sleep.

4 1 had seen ('d seen)   2 has seen ('s seen)

5 1 had (already) finished
2 had eaten
3 learned
4 never
5 had (ever) stayed

Reading p.95

1 A   2 B   3 B

Note: 1 This could be a notice in the street or in a public place such as a park. 2 You would find this notice near a moving staircase. 3 This is a personal note.

Listening p.96

1 B   2 C   3 B   4 B   5 A   6 A   7 C

Tapescript

1 *What is Susan going to wear?*

S: *What do you think I should wear – this long skirt and a jumper, or a short skirt and shirt?*

A: *Well, we're going walking, so I think you'd be better in jeans than a skirt – and a warm jumper. You don't want to get cold.*

S: *Oh, OK.*

2 *Where does George live?*

G: *Come round and see us sometime – we live in North Street – number 11.*

A: *Oh, is that the house with the balcony and the separate garage?*

G: *No ... it's got a garage, but it's joined onto the house. And there's no balcony.*

3 *What are Kevin and Sally going to do tonight?*

K: *What shall we do tonight? It's a bit cold to go out.*

S: *There's a good film on TV .... or we could have a game of cards. Or I'm quite happy just reading.*

K: *Let's watch the film. I've got nothing to read, and I always lose at cards.*

4 *What is Sarah going to buy?*

J: *I really like your new curtains. Great colour! They look good with the armchair, and the carpet. And are the cushions new too?*

S: *No, I've had them for a long time. But actually I'm getting some new ones. I'd really like a new coffee table too, but I can't afford it.*

5 *Which picture are they looking at?*

A: *That's a lovely picture – is it your family?*

B: *Yes, my friend painted it for me. That's my father, that's my mother – and that's me with my little brother.*

A: *Yes, I can see that you haven't changed at all!*

6 *What present has Christine bought for the baby?*

C: *My sister's got a new baby daughter and I bought this ... do you think she'll like it? I wanted to get a toy rabbit but they were all so expensive. And I thought this would be useful.*

A: *Oh, she'll love it. Look at the rabbit on the front, it's sweet.*

C: *Well you do need lots of clothes for a new baby. But I really wanted to get a toy, all the same.*

7 *What is the man going to buy?*

A: *I'll get something for lunch while I'm in the supermarket. Shall I get some fish?*

B: *We had fish and chips yesterday. Why don't you get some chicken and salad?*

A: *OK, I'll get some salad but I'd prefer pizza to chicken.*

B: *That's fine. Whatever you like.*

Writing p.97

Example answer

Dear Lorna

Thanks for your letter; it was great to hear from you. Well, you asked me to tell you about where I live, so I'll do my best. I live in a small town in the south of the country. There are lots of things to do – there are sports facilities, and a cinema. As well as that there are interesting shops, so I often go shopping with friends. I really enjoy living here. What I like most is the people, who are really friendly.

Well, that's all I have time to write now. Keep in touch.

Love

Naomi

UNIT 12

Vocabulary p.98

1 *Across:* 1 midnight   6 sheet   8 body   10 scream
12 go   14 funny   16 magic   17 to
Down: 2 nasty   3 ghost   4 true   5 blood   7 try
9 faint   10 so   11 him   13 by   15 no

2 1 frightening   2 astonished   3 amusing
4 interesting   5 bored   6 amazing   7 disgusting
8 embarrassed

3 1 love story   2 science fiction   3 detective story
4 horror story   5 adventure story   6 thriller

Tapescript

1

A: *In the book I'm reading at present, a girl meets the boy of her dreams but their families don't get on and they have to leave one another – it's so sad.*

2

B: *I'm reading about a group of people who travel into space and discover a new world with very strange people on it.*

3

C: *I'm halfway through a book about a murder – there's a policeman trying to find out who committed the crime. There are lots of people who could have done it, but I think I know who did!*

4

D: *I'm reading a really frightening story – it's about a family who come to live in an old house, and strange things start to happen, and they realise there must be a ghost or something in the house. I haven't finished it yet but I think something really nasty's going to happen at the end. It's not the sort of book you want to read at night on your own.*

5

E: *I'm reading a book about two boys who find a cave, and they go down there, then there's an accident and they can't get out – but one of them has an idea for a way of escaping. It's brilliant.*

6

F: *My book's about a man who's trying to find the answer to a secret – a mystery – and he thinks he's being followed by someone, but he doesn't know who. I can't wait to see how it ends!*

Listening p.99

1 1 church   2 nervous people   3 bat   4 victim
   5 £1.95   6 fish and chips

Tapescript

In the final series of 'About Britain' we visit the fishing town and port of Whitby, on the east coast of England. For almost fifteen hundred years, as far as we know, there has been a town and church here and so the town has lots of history. But one particular reason why many people come to Whitby is because of its connection with the story of Dracula. There's even a special centre you can visit called The Dracula Experience, *but it's not for nervous people! As the story goes, Count Dracula's boat, the* Demeter, *came to Whitby in a terrible storm. The only thing found alive on board was a black dog, which escaped off the boat and disappeared in the churchyard. Then strange things started to happen … It's well worth a visit to see terrifying electronic models of the main events of the story including Dracula changing from a man to a bat, and the beautiful Lucy who is his victim and who comes back to life in the form of a vampire before she is finally laid to rest. This interactive centre, for both children and adults, is on the Sea Front facing the harbour, It's £1.95 for adults and £1.00 for children.*

After your visit, you can climb the steps – people say there are 199 of them – to the churchyard of St Mary's Church, where some of the most frightening events of the story are set. And then, if you are feeling hungry after so much excitement, we recommend the Magpie Café, facing the harbour, which is said to have the best fish and chips in England.

2 *Example answer*

> Dear Chris
> We are in Whitby. Today I went to a place called 'The Dracula Experience'. It was quite good because you could find out what happened when Dracula came to Whitby. Next we're going to eat fish and chips.
> See you soon.
> Love
> Peter

Reading p.100

1 C (the text is a book review)
2 D (he imagined the whole story while sitting … in the very same hotel)
3 A (One of those … novels that can burn itself into your brain)
4 C (The heart of the book is … the way Jack and Danny feel about each other)
5 B (The story is seen through the eyes of a five-year-old boy)

Grammar p.101

1 1 There   2 It   3 It   4 There   5 There   6 It

2 1 is difficult   2 It is, to   3 It is hard   4 was, find
   5 is sleeping   6 There are, waiting

4 1 there are
   2 the first time
   3 very interesting.
   4 Do you want
   5 as long as

Reading p.102

1 B   2 D   3 B   4 B   5 D   6 C   7 A   8 D   9 C
10 A

Reading p.102

1 B   2 C

Note: 1 You would find this in a theatre advertisement or brochure. 2 This is from a film advertisement.

Writing p.103

1 b   2 a   3 d   4 c

Example answer

It was midnight. The moon shone over the quiet town. The cold wind from the sea blew down the empty streets. Everyone was sleeping – except for one person wrapped in a black coat, who was slowly climbing the hill from the harbour.

He stopped outside a house and turned the door handle. It wouldn't open. The face of a woman appeared at the window above. 'Who are you? What do you want?' she called. He looked up and his face shone white in the moonlight, but his hands were red with blood. Then he gave the door one last push and it opened. He went inside.

PRACTICE EXAM

Reading Part 1 p.106

1 C   2 A   3 B   4 C   5 C

Reading Part 2 p.108

6 E   7 D   8 F   9 B   10 G

Reading Part 3 p.110

11 A   12 B   13 A   14 A   15 B   16 B   17 B   18 A   19 B   20 A

Reading Part 4 p.112

21 D   22 C   23 B   24 A   25 C

Reading Part 5 p.114

26 C   27 B   28 A   29 B   30 A   31 C   32 C   33 D   34 C   35 A

Writing Part 1 p.115

1 the first time (Not *It is my first time to …*)
2 I think
3 as warm/hot as
4 me to go
5 enjoying

Writing Part 2 p.116

6 *Example answer*

To: Stephanie
From: Janis
Hi Stephanie! Thank you for my beautiful scarf –
I love it! It's the perfect colour for my new coat.
I enjoyed my birthday very much. I went out to the cinema with some friends. It was fun!
Best wishes
Janis

Writing Part 3 p.117

7 *Example answer*

Dear Paola,

Thank you for your letter – it was nice to hear from you. I hope that you are enjoying going to your new sports club!

I enjoy sports too. I like playing hockey – I play every Tuesday evening with friends. My favourite sport is football. I'm not very good at it, but I like watching other people playing. I try to go every week to watch my local team. I want to learn to play golf so I am thinking about joining my local golf club.

Tell me more about your sports club!

I'm looking forward to hearing from you soon.
Best wishes,

Juan

8 *Example answer*

A happy day

One day I wanted to go to the beach. I phoned my friends but they were busy and couldn't come, so I went by myself. When I got there the beach was crowded, but I found a small space and sat down. The sun was shining and it was hot, but I was feeling lonely. Then a girl came up to me and said 'Sue! Do you remember me?' I remembered her face but not her name – then suddenly I recognised her. Ten years ago we were good friends, but then she moved to another town. We talked for hours, and it was a very happy day after all.

Listening Part 1 p.118

1 B   2 A   3 C   4 A   5 B   6 A   7 C

Tapescript

Example: *What time does the performance begin?*

A: *What time should we eat? Before the theatre or after?*

B: *Well, it doesn't start until half past eight, so I reckon we have time to eat before that. Let's see … we need to pick up the tickets at about eight, so let's say about six thirty? If we finish by half past seven that should leave us plenty of time.*

1   *What is the man's job now?*

W: *Haven't you just changed your job?*

M: *Yes, and I'm really enjoying it. You're more free than on the buses … you don't have a timetable, and you drive all over the place, and you can talk to the people you pick up. But it's not what I'd really like to do.*

W: *Oh? What's that?*

M: *Well, actually I'm saving up to train as a pilot … that's my dream.*

2   *What will the woman post?*

M: *If you're going out, could you post a letter for me, please?*

W: *Yes, of course. I've got to go to the post office myself. I've had a parcel from my friend in Japan and I've written her a postcard to thank her. So it's no problem for me to post your letter at the same time.*

3   *What kind of holiday is the man going to have?*

W: *So what are you going to do on your holiday this year? I thought you were going walking.*

M: *Yes, I am. I've already booked the ticket. I'm going on a trip in the Spanish mountains. Last year I went on a beach holiday but it was a bit boring – I like a bit more action. I did think about a skiing holiday in the winter instead, but I do like the sun.*

4   *Why does the man need to see the doctor?*

M: *I've got an appointment with the doctor tomorrow so I'll be a bit late.*

W: *Oh … you're not still getting those headaches, are you? Or is it your stomach again?*

M: *No, actually I've been getting these pains in my knee every time I play tennis. My sister had something similar and she ended up having to have an operation on her back – so I thought I should see the doctor about it.*

5   *What does the boy decide to buy?*

W: *What are you going to buy with the money your aunt gave you for your birthday?*

B: *IWell, she suggested a book but I've already got a whole lot I haven't read yet. So I might get a CD or something.*

W: *Mmm. Or a video?*

B: *It's better to borrow them. I might get a computer game … but I don't think I've got enough money for a good one. No, I'd rather have music. Then you can listen lots of times.*

6   *Which is the girl's room?*

G: *My new room's OK, I suppose. The old one did have a television, and I miss that a lot, but this one's got a proper wardrobe for my clothes. And I don't like doing* *homework in my bedroom so I don't need a desk – or a table next to the bed. I never read in bed anyway.*

7 *What is the man having a problem with at present?*
w: *You look a bit depressed – what's the matter?*
M: *Oh, it's just one thing after another … everything in the house seems to be breaking down – and it's all so expensive to get mended. Last week it was the fridge, and I've only just got the TV fixed. And this morning the computer wouldn't work at all. It's probably something quite easy to fix, but I can't do it – I'll have to take it back to the shop. And my wife's got the car so I can't do anything until she gets home from work.*

Listening Part 2 p.120

8 C   9 C   10 C   11 A   12 C   13 B

Tapescript

Welcome to Radio North and What's On This Weekend. *And this weekend, why not pay a visit to the Chelford summer festival? As usual, it will be held on the second weekend in July, and this year's festival is going to be very special as it's the tenth anniversary. It will start on Friday afternoon, that's Friday the 7th, and finish on Saturday evening, July 8th.*

So on Friday afternoon our very own Jody Player from Radio North will be in Chelford market place to open the festival. You've heard her introducing Songs of the Week *on the radio for the past two years – now's your chance to see what she looks like! There will also be speeches from local people, including the well-known actress Mandy George, and music and fun for everyone, from 4.00 to 7.00 p.m.*

After that the action moves to the village hall where there will be a buffet meal at only £6.00 each followed by a quiz night – you have the chance to win a free weekend for two in a luxury hotel in London as the main prize, and other wonderful prizes include free membership of the local sports club and free weekly cinema tickets for a whole year – imagine, seeing a different film every weekend for a whole year for nothing! So if you're feeling lucky, book for the meal and quiz night now.

On Saturday there will be a funfair on the sports field with lots for the children to do, and there will also be stalls selling home-made food including the famous Chelford lemon curd. 'Curd' is an old name for cream cheese, but lemon curd isn't actually made of cheese at all – it's just eggs, lemon and sugar cooked together until they make a sort of jam. You buy it in jars and can eat it on bread or with cake – it's a traditional English food.

In the afternoon from 2.00 to 5.00 there will be sports competitions and games, and then in the evening there will be a special dinner with meat cooked over an open

fire, salads and baked potatoes, and an ice-cream dessert with five different varieties including strawberry, orange and chocolate.

The meal costs £8.00 per person and as you eat, you can listen to Joe Stanton's old time band. Then, if you have any energy left, there will be a disco with live music from local group The Shout *until midnight.*

Listening Part 3 p.121

14 Pieter   15 alone   16 closed   17 sun-cream
18 dark   19 9.30

Tapescript

Hello everyone, and I'd like to welcome you all here for your holiday with Ski Holidays Unlimited. I'm your tour leader and my name's Pieter – that's P I E T E R – and I'm here to make sure you don't have any problems. In fact I'm sure you're all going to have a wonderful time – we've got perfect snow conditions this week – but while you're all here I'd just like to go over a few safety rules. First of all, and the most important rule – never, ever go skiing alone. If you do and you fall or injure yourself, you're in trouble. Always make sure there's at least one other person with you – preferably more. And if you're skiing with friends who maybe aren't as good as you, don't encourage them to do more than they're happy with. Skiing should be safe and fun for everyone in the group. Now, as I said, we've got very good snow conditions this week, but things can change quickly and if the snow starts to melt some ski runs may be closed for safety reasons. So please don't try to ski there as this can put both you and other people in danger. I'm sure I don't need to tell you that when you're up on the mountain you must have warm clothing. But at the same time the sun can be very strong up here, so make sure you have sun-cream for your face so that you don't get burnt. And finally, even if you're having a wonderful time, remember to allow yourself time to get off the mountain before dark, or you could be in real trouble. Right, I'll be here in the hotel reception every morning from 9.30 if you have any problems or questions and in the meantime – happy skiing.

Listening Part 4 p.122

20 A   21 A   22 B   23 B   24 B   25 A

Tapescript

JIM: *Megan – I thought you must be ill. You missed the class.*
MEGAN: *Yeah, I had to go to the dentist.*
J: *Yeah, well actually quite a few people were away. I think a lot of people have got colds. It was a pity*

because Mrs Bleikdale was telling us about those talks we have to give.

M: What talks?

J: You know, she said at the beginning of term. We have to give a talk with a partner about a book we've read. The first one's next week … next Wednesday.

M: Oh, I don't remember her telling us anything about that.

J: She did, right on the first day. You were there!

M: Anyway, at least I won't have to do it next week 'cos I wasn't there today.

J: Er … don't be too sure about that.

M: What?

J: Yeah, well, I said I'd do it first 'cos I'd rather get it out of the way, and then no-one else wanted to do it, so then Mrs Bleikdale suggested you … and I didn't think you'd mind so I said OK, I'd tell you.

M: Oh Jim – and I've got a maths test on Friday!

J: So have I. Don't worry. It's only a ten-minute talk, after all.

M: Well, what do we have to do exactly?

J: I said. It's just a ten-minute talk about a book.

M: What, any book?

J: I suppose so.

M: So we just tell the story?

J: Well … and she said we have to decide whether we'd recommend it and why …

M: Well, that depends on the person, doesn't it? Anyway, I suppose we'd better choose a book. I dunno … you like thrillers, don't you?

J: Well, I used to, but I haven't read any for a while. Anyway, we want something we both like.

M: Well, I read this really good book recently called Northern Lights – it's a sort of mixture of history and magic and travel.

J: Oh, yes, my brother says that's great – he's just reading it – but it's long.

M: Go on, you read fast. I'd really like to do that – get it from your brother for the weekend. It's going to rain all weekend anyway.

J: OK, so we'll go with that.